It's one thing to say [...]ng biblical and persona[...] [...]ge readers to choose to put God's "amazing, limitless love [...] [...]ove brought a message of hope," and so do these timely devotionals—a hope that we can change the world one small act of love at a time!

—Gloria Willoughby, MTS
Manager of Crossroads 24/7 Prayer Centre
PAOC Minister
www.crossroads.ca/247prayer

The heart of the Father is woven for each of us throughout this devotional. I was brought to tears more than once! It both encouraged and challenged me, from the life stories and personal applications to the prayer at the end of each page. Get it, read it, and apply it!

—Penny Lane
Former Pastor at *Catch the Fire*

Ruth Teakle digs deep into our hearts, confronting issues we all grapple with: Can I be honest enough to ask for a miracle? Can God use me above and beyond my limitations? Skillfully drawing from scriptural accounts and personal reflections, Ruth and contributors call us to greater faith. I was informed but all the more blessed. Keep a pen nearby—there's lots you'll want to note!

—Susan Wells
Author, Speaker

This book is biblically sound, encouraging, and inspirational. The author writes as *"an example to the believers in word, in conduct, in love, in spirit, in faith in purity"* (1 Timothy 4:12). She invites us to choose love in all situations, for the love of God indwelling us and shared with others will never fail.

—Shirley Ratcliff, Major (R)
The Salvation Army—Canada and Bermuda Territory

Choosing Love

Choosing Love

A 30 Day Devotional Journey

Ruth Teakle
& a Company of Friends

CHOOSING LOVE
Copyright © 2021 by Ruth Teakle

All rights reserved. Neither this publication nor any part of this publication may be reproduced or transmitted in any form or by any means, electronic or mechanical, including photocopying, recording or any information storage and retrieval system, without permission in writing from the author.

Unless otherwise indicated, scripture quotations are taken from the Holy Bible, NEW INTERNATIONAL VERSION®, NIV® Copyright © 1973, 1978, 1984, 2011 by Biblica, Inc.® Used by permission. All rights reserved worldwide. Scripture quotations marked (AMP) are taken from the Amplified® Bible, Copyright © 1954, 1958, 1962, 1964, 1965, 1987 by The Lockman Foundation. Used by permission. Scripture quotations marked (MSG) are taken from The Message. Copyright © by Eugene H. Peterson 1993, 1994, 1995, 1996, 2000, 2001, 2002. Used by permission of NavPress Publishing Group. Scripture quotations marked (ESV) are taken from The Holy Bible, English Standard Version® (ESV®), copyright © 2001 by Crossway, a publishing ministry of Good News Publishers. Used by permission. All rights reserved. Scripture quotations marked (NKJV) are taken from the New King James Version®. Copyright © 1982 by Thomas Nelson, Inc. Used by permission. All rights reserved. Scripture quotations marked (NLT) are taken from the Holy Bible, New Living Translation, copyright ©1996, 2004, 2007 by Tyndale House Foundation. Used by permission of Tyndale House Publishers, Inc., Carol Stream, Illinois 60188. All rights reserved. Scripture quotations marked (TPT) are taken from The Passion Translation®. Copyright © 2017, 2018 by Passion & Fire Ministries, Inc. Used by permission. All rights reserved. ThePassionTranslation.com. Scripture quotations marked (NASB) are taken from the New American Standard Bible®, Copyright © 1960, 1962, 1963, 1968, 1971, 1972, 1973, 1975, 1977, 1995 by The Lockman Foundation. Used by permission.

Printed in Canada

Print ISBN: 978-1-4866-2137-8
eBook ISBN: 978-1-4866-2138-5

Word Alive Press
119 De Baets Street, Winnipeg, MB R2J 3R9
www.wordalivepress.ca

Cataloguing in Publication may be obtained through Library and Archives Canada

Contents

	Getting Started	ix
Day 1:	Love without Limits	1
Day 2:	Rescued by Love	3
Day 3:	Unfailing Love	5
Day 4:	Making Room	7
Day 5:	You Are Loved	9
Day 6:	Drawn by Love	11
Day 7:	Extravagant Love	13
Day 8:	God's Court	15
Day 9:	The Imprint of Love	17
Day 10:	Loving God and Letting Go	19
Day 11:	Will You Be a Neighbour?	21
Day 12:	When You Long for One More Gift	23
Day 13:	A Labour of Love	25
Day 14:	Love Stirs the Nest	27
Day 15:	Living Out an Endless Love	29
Day 16:	The Power of His Love	33
Day 17:	Lost and Alone and Longing for Love	35
Day 18:	The Sacrifice of Love	37
Day 19:	As a Mother Loves Her Children	39
Day 20:	Refreshing Love	41
Day 21:	Love Unsolicited	43
Day 22:	Love's Surprise	45
Day 23:	His Forever Love	47
Day 24:	The Bedrock of Love	49
Day 25:	You've Always Loved	51
Day 26:	A Father's Love	53

Day 27:	Dr. Luke's Lesson on Love (with a Twist)	55
Day 28:	Love Sees More	57
Day 29:	Held by Love	59
Day 30:	The Father Stepped In	61
	Small Group Helps	63
	Contributors	69
	About the Author	75

Getting Started

But the fruit produced by the Holy Spirit within you is divine love in all its varied expressions: *joy that overflows, peace that subdues, patience that endures, kindness in action, a life full of virtue, faith that prevails, gentleness of heart, and strength of spirit… they are meant to be limitless.*
—Galatians 5:22–23a TPT (emphasis added)

In the Western world when we say the word "love," we can mean many different things. I can love my cat, my wife, my car, my pillow, my job, my music, or my new haircut. But hopefully I don't love all of them in the same way! Music, books, blogs, ads all talk about love—you may have it, want it, be finding it on the latest match-making site, or have just lost it.

Biblical love is much less confusing. There are mainly two aspects of biblical love: *phileo*, which includes appreciation and deep care for another, and *agape*, the higher sacrificial love that can also love an enemy. Interestingly, the Greek translation of the biblical instruction to *"be devoted to one another in love"* uses the Greek word *Philadelphia* in instructing us to love our neighbours as if they were our brothers (Romans 12:10a). When Jesus cried at the grave of Lazarus, one witness spoke of His love for Lazarus by using a derivative of the word *phileo* when he said, *"See how He loved him!"* (John 11:36b). I best understand *phileo* as a kind of love that reaches out of my heart to the heart or the need of another "as though" they were family—my brothers or sisters. I see it in Jonathan and David (1 Samuel 18:1–3), where their souls were "knit" together.

In *Choosing Love*, we are focusing on testimonies and biblical events in which *phileo*, brotherly love, and *agape*, the highest form of Christian love, are demonstrated. *Agape* refers to a love that God *is* (1 John 4:8,16) and the love that God *shows* (John 3:16; 1 John 4:9). His love toward us restores, forgives, heals, saves, transforms, strengthens, protects, and blesses. It's no better displayed than in John 3:16, which says, *"For God so loved ("agapaō") the world, that he gave his one and only Son, that whoever believes in him should not perish but have eternal life."*

It seems reasonable to consider that Paul in his letter to the Philippians focused on love first because love mirrors the nature of God. God is love. He knew that if the Philippians' love abounded, they would be well on the way to Christian maturity. Jesus said that *"everyone will know"* that we are His disciples if we love one another (John 13:35), so this love in action is evidence of the goodness of God to others inside our homes, inside the church, and outside in our world. When we love God's way, we show the world that we're different. Agape identifies the fruit of the spirit in the life of a believer—divine (agape) love *in all its varied* expressions. It's the evidence that the Holy Spirit is working in one's life, growing us God's way.

Biblical love is volitional and intentional, a divine love—we choose to love. It's a selfless love characterized by servanthood, humility, compassion, patience, sacrifice, kindness, and consistency. It is not based on attraction, reluctant duty, or sentiment. It chooses to see what God sees, acts without regard to personal inconvenience, and looks for good beneath the surface.

In 1 Corinthians 13:4–8a, Paul gives us a well-defined picture of agape love:

> *Love is patient, love is kind. It does not envy, it does not boast, it is not proud. It does not dishonor others, it is not self-seeking, it is not easily angered, it keeps no record of wrongs. Love does not delight in evil but rejoices with the truth. It always protects, always trusts, always hopes, always perseveres. Love never fails.*

As you work through this devotional, you'll revisit some of the great Bible personalities who chose love—some who gave it, some who received it, and some who nourished it to fulfilment. You'll also be invited into very vulnerable and personal moments in the lives of some beautiful, dedicated, victorious, and well-practised lovers of God and people.

It's my prayer that you will be stirred by the Holy Spirit to invite His work in a new way in your life so that you can enjoy even greater expressions of love bubbling out from a heart that is passionately in love with Him.

I have included a brief prayer at the end of each reading. Please take a few minutes to meditate on His love during each prayer as He whispers to you through the scriptures or the narratives on this thirty-day journey.

Love without Limits
Day One

But the fruit produced by the Holy Spirit within you is divine love in all its varied expressions... these qualities... are meant to be limitless.
—Galatians 5:22–23. TPT (emphasis added)

Every eye in the house was on Jesus that day, and every ear was attuned to His teaching. Teachers of the law had come from every town of Galilee, Judea, and Jerusalem. In this uncommon crowd of theologians, the presence of God was there to heal. Luke records it in this manner:

> *Then behold, men brought on a bed a man who was paralyzed ... And when they could not find how they might bring him in, because of the crowd, they went up on the housetop and let him down with his bed through the tiling into the midst before Jesus. When He saw their faith, He said to him, "Man, your sins are forgiven you." And the scribes and the Pharisees began to reason, saying, "Who is this who speaks blasphemies? Who can forgive sins but God alone?" But when Jesus perceived their thoughts, He answered ... "the Son of Man has power on earth to forgive sins"—He said to the man who was paralyzed, "I say to you, arise, take up your bed, and go to your house." Immediately he rose up before them ... and departed to his own house ...*
> —Luke 5:18–25, NKJV

For the four friends, getting their paralytic friend to Jesus required both persistence and ingenuity. They had already carried the sick man through the jostling crowd to no avail, so they had to find an alternative access point to the place where Jesus was teaching. The houses at the time would have been built of stone with flat roofs made of a thick mud and straw mix. The best option was the roof, but to reach it they would have to carry him, on his bed, up some narrow, probably twisting, steps. They'd need to tear apart a stranger's roof, carve out a man-sized hole, and lower the man on his bed into the midst of a focused crowd.

They were compelled by their compassionate love for this man and a confidence in Jesus' power to heal. Sometimes loving others fiercely involves heavy lifting, inconvenience, and personal risk. It means facing the obstacles that might prevent one from getting to Jesus. The friends in Luke's Gospel were single-minded and devoted in their quest.

What sets this miracle apart in Jesus' ministry is that it wasn't the paralytic, who was both forgiven and healed by Jesus, at the centre of attention but the four friends who, with unwavering resolve, brought the man to Jesus. "*When He saw their faith ...*" (v. 20), He responded to the man's needs. This miracle is all about the persevering faith, kindness, and love of friends who recognized the power of His presence. These men believed on his behalf. Many would have given up, hoping for a "next time," perhaps waiting outside hoping to grab His attention as He exited the house. But these were four dedicated, caring friends with radical faith.

How willing are you to help carry, in love, those paralyzed by life without judging them? What roof would you be willing to wreck if you knew you were in His presence and He was ready to forgive and heal? What heavy lifting would you be willing to do for a friend? May the Lord give each of us the kind of love whose outworking is kindness, perseverance, and an unshakeable faith for those around us who need our help to get to Jesus.

Dear Lord, stir my heart to be bold in faith for your heart towards those around me. Teach me how to walk with an unwavering resolve with my eyes wide open to Heaven's agenda. Amen.

Rescued by Love
Day Two

Let no debt remain outstanding, except the continuing debt to love one another...
—Romans 13:8a

Our small white-washed, stucco cottage sat at the end of a narrow laneway across from the new local school. The laneway was bordered by long grass and was often strewn with empty beer bottles. It was quiet during the day, aside from a few big barking dogs. On weekends, the lonely and despairing of the town would often need a place to sit down and finish a few extras. It wasn't uncommon to come into the driveway and have to pass by one or two curled up in the long grass with their partially-finished bottles.

Mom was short in stature, but she was exceptionally tall in love and compassion. She believed that there was good in everyone and that some people just needed a little help along the way. She seemed to see something of the "God" vision for people's lives.

It wasn't unexpected on those weekend nights to be told we would be donating a bedroom for a "guest." Mom's idea of a guest was somebody who would stagger up the front step, steadied by her arm, and stumble onto a chair in the kitchen. There, a triple strength coffee and an onion sandwich would sit ready, followed by a night in the "guest" room where they could safely sleep it off. Dad gave reluctant permission, but Mom was fearless. Bad language or a dishevelled appearance never disqualified anyone from roadside service with a smile.

The next morning when they were sobered up, Mom would share the salvation message and remind them that God had a greater purpose for them than sitting in laneways and drowning their pain in substantial amounts of alcohol. She took time to listen to their struggles—they never mocked her, argued, or pushed her aside. Compelling love drew them into a place of gratitude and consideration.

Mom knew how to live out love, and it paid off. There were unforgettable and unique stories of some of those guys who were turned around by accepting God's offer and eating Marjorie's onion sandwiches. One of them I remember well. After a few repeated rescue encounters, he attended the Salvation Army Harbour Light for rehabilitation at Mom's recommendation. He turned his life around, began a relationship with the Lord, and was restored into the workforce. He had no problem sharing his story of those "God encounters" in Marjorie's kitchen when he was elected mayor of the town, a position he held for three terms.

I often think of how much Mom was like Jesus. He was always willing to meet people where they were at—in their laneways of life. For Jesus, there was Bartimaeus, Zacchaeus, the woman with the issue of blood, the demon-possessed man, and the crippled woman. He took them from blindness to sight, from a tree of deception to a table of forgiveness, from the distress of infirmity to healing and health. Sometimes your condition contradicts the position Heaven has planned for you. Because of one thing that's wrong, everything else in your life shuts down. Until he met Jesus, Bartimaeus sat by the roadside begging, simply surviving in a society that ignored his affliction. He couldn't fix what was broken.

The men in the laneway had their bottles because they couldn't fix what was broken in their lives. It was the comfort for what they couldn't correct. But love brought the opportunity for something greater. Love brought the good news that someone cared. Love brought a message of hope that verified change was possible through Jesus. God's love—amazing, limitless, persistent, and full of hope—is available to rescue me every day. I'm in!

Jesus, the Word tells me that on the cross you paid a debt for me that I could never pay. Your righteousness and your love covered me. Soften my heart to prepare me to meet others in the laneways of their lives. Let me see what you see, and love like you love.

Unfailing Love

Day Three

Contributed by Peggy Kennedy

"Since you are precious and honored in my sight, and because I love you…"
—Isaiah 43:4a

There's something about dysfunction, even from a childhood experience, that can leave you with a distorted image of God … and of His love for us. I certainly "knew" He loved me, but I also depreciated my worth and minimized my eligibility for being blessed by the Lord. I could enthusiastically commend others and even convince others of the Lord's love; however, I would respond to any compliment paid to me by diminishing and discounting it: "Oh, this dress? I found it at the thrift store!"

Gideon's story in Judges 6 tells of his responses to the Lord that revealed his distorted images of God and himself. Though chosen of God for a national assignment, he really needed a transforming encounter. My own distorted conclusions confined me to marginalized thinking. Like Gideon, I often contradicted what I heard from the Lord. I was sure that miracles were not intended for me. Yes, self-disqualification gets very loud but often masquerades in other ways. Sometimes I would weep and repent of envying the seeming advantage other people had!

It wasn't until I was over forty-years-old that truth began to penetrate through the faulty lens. Soon I would discover more deeply buried family secrets—and they do go deep! How tenderly His voice began to fill in the gaps. Those encounters brought fresh understanding. As I was being healed, I yearned for more! Knowing you're worthy of love frees you from performance and perfectionism.

In the weeks before the release of my first book, a friend gifted me the opportunity to meet with a Spirit-led counsellor. As he led me to Isaiah 43:4, I had a vision of myself receiving a beautiful doll from my grade two teacher. In the vision, I was reliving that wonderful memory when she had given me a treasured doll that year. I had cherished it as it adorned my pillow and warmed my heart.

The vision, however, included what I wouldn't have known at age eight. In the vision, the Lord was standing behind the teacher—looking over her head and making eye-contact with me. In the vision, she couldn't see Him, but I certainly could! The Lord spoke: "I told her to do that!" Six words, but they conveyed so much affirmation. Her "just because" gift to me was neither a reward nor even an incentive. It was an expression of the Lord's heart through her kindness. Love was doing its transforming work!

The Lord has so faithfully continued to build on the incremental healing He has performed. The distorted images are continuing to be replaced not just by information about the Lord but by revelation and lived experience. Verses such as Isaiah 43:4, reminding me that I am precious and honoured in His sight, have become engraved on my heart. I have come to know a love that heals, a love that refreshes, a love that frees, a love that transforms. That love brings confidence in who I am in the Lord and of His assignments. I no longer need to envy the open doors the Lord gives to others, nor minimize mine! And it's no surprise that I keep Psalm 143:8a written out and available as I begin my day: *"Let the morning bring me word of your unfailing love …"*

Thank you, Lord, for reminding me that I am precious in your sight, cherished, affirmed, and loved without restriction. When I'm tempted to disqualify myself, open my eyes again that I might see your love engraved upon my heart.

Making Room
Day Four

"Above all, keep fervent in your love for one another..."
—I Peter 4:8a, NASB

Baking some muffins, cleaning the main floor, rearranging the chairs, retrieving the china cups and saucers from the cabinet—I had many details to care for before the sixteen women from my weekly Bible study would arrive. Nevertheless, I relished the opportunity to make room for this intergenerational group of women because I treasured the relationships we'd been building over our weeks together.

The Shunammite woman (2 Kings 4:8–17) may have felt similarly about Elisha's visits. Elisha's work was supported and strengthened by her act of love. Love was the source. Sometimes it presented as hospitality, sometimes as kindness, sometimes as generosity—but the source was God's endless love. She had watched Elisha pass by many times; she had shared the food from her table, and she knew she was responding to God's tug. Travelling prophets were dependent upon random hospitality, and this Shunamite woman, recognizing Elisha's need for rest and quietness, made room for him.

Imagine her preparing that room on the roof—placing one table, a bed, one chair, and a small candle stand. (Sadly, no record of muffins or china cups.) The room became a solemn place of retreat and restoration, a place where the prophet could listen and meditate. It was there to bring blessing to the man of God.

On one of the visits, Elisha was particularly filled with gratitude and determined to bless this woman and her husband in return. What the

Shunamite woman didn't know was that God was about to dig up a long-buried dream. She responded to Elisha's offer of choosing a thank you gift by saying, "I dwell among my own people." This translates to "I am content; there's nothing that I need."

Elisha pursued the ask, but she wasn't ready to share the secret ache in her soul—that she had no children, no son to carry on the family name. Elisha prophesied to her that about this time next year, she would hold a son in her arms. Her response to the word of the Lord? Very much like ours. "Oh no, that can't happen. I'm OK. Stop taunting me. Leave things be!" Cleary the fulfillment of this prophecy was beyond her comfort zone, and she was uncertain of its interruption.

How many times does God bring an opportunity our way to be loved or blessed by Him and we just say, "Oh no, I'm fine"? Even though we're enjoying our present blessings, God often wants to bless us with more. This woman wasn't immune to the heartache of her broken world, but she maintained her faith and, even in her hesitancy, gave God the last word. God fulfilled His promise to the Shunammite woman, and she held a treasured son in her arms the next year.

The Shunamite's miraculous story would never have happened had she not been willing to show love to a passerby and make room for his presence. God invites us to give love and make room for Him. I've seen many times in my life when God has enlarged His presence in me when I've allowed His love to leak out in little ways and in hidden places. In unheralded venues. In insignificant events. In church nurseries with crying babies needing comfort. In long prayer lines and crowded grocery lines. Through rearranged chairs and fresh muffins.

When the motivation of the heart brings no self gain, get ready for Him to pour His love back into you in ways you never expected. Keep sharing His love, make room for His presence, and yes, at some point He may breathe life onto a long-buried dream!

Father, I'm giving you the last word. I repent for deciding when you are finished with my dreams. Today I make room. I open my heart to your presence in a greater way. Keep my motives pure and my heart ready to be blessed and to be a blessing.

You Are Loved

Day Five

Contributed by Wendy Hagar

"Love never fails…these three remain: faith, hope and love. But the greatest of these is love."

—I Corinthians 13:8a,13a

In 1999, something not easily explained began to burn in my heart—a longing that I knew was being seeded from Heaven to know how I could make a tangible difference in the lives of people. I can only describe it as a fire of love that wasn't fueled by big ideas, committee meetings, or flashy promises. With it came a new sense of searching for God's purpose for my life with a new precision and passion. I knew detours could happen, as they happen to many when they chase all the wrong things—money, success, social climbing. All things that would never satisfy. It wasn't that I wasn't on track to do my best for Him, but this call of the Spirit left me hungry for something more.

It was close to Easter, so I undertook a (safe) forty-day fast. I could never have dreamed of what God was up to in me and how far-reaching His invitation to love others would take me. Within months, at a Sunday church service, I felt the fire begin to burn again. I listened to a missionary's story of an orphanage in Russia with forty naked babies. As I made my donation in the offering, I heard the Lord say, "I'm requiring more of you in missions." I froze, as He was writing on my heart the needs of the "forgotten children."

Before the end of the day, I committed to Him that I would make clothes for these children and others. In the flesh it was daunting and unnerving—but God! My goal was threefold: to complete one hundred pairs of pyjamas for infants, to sew one hundred cloth gift bags, and to knit one hundred pairs of mittens. God had filled my heart with love to make a difference for one hundred of His forgotten children. It was a John 3:16 fresh revelation: "...*God so loved the world that he gave*..." No one should ever feel they don't matter. The cross is proof of God's never-ending love, and I considered my opportunity to give simply an expression of His beautiful sacrifice in giving His life for me.

Well, just like He multiplied the loaves and fishes, He multiplied my gift to Him. That small beginning took over my home as volunteers by the dozen began to come to help. Word spread—God was in it—and we received hundreds of dollars of donations, unsolicited gifts, and practical help from service groups, churches, and individual donors who had caught the vision.

And here I am in 2021, managing and running an international humanitarian organization, Sew on Fire—evangelism through humanitarian aid. Constantly ballooning efforts have brought us to a nine-thousand-square-foot warehouse with volunteers from across the region. Since the year 2000, over 350,000 gift bags have been distributed to over one hundred countries, working with over 350 other Canadian registered charities enabling children to go to school and bringing hope and help to hurting and often forgotten men and women. "You are Loved." This short but powerful message is fastened to every gift bag we send.

It's true that little becomes much when God is in it. What can I possibly ever give Jesus but my heart? Second Chronicles 16:9 says, "*For the eyes of the Lord run to and fro throughout the whole earth, to show Himself strong on behalf of those whose heart is loyal to Him*" (NKJV). His love has always been meant to be given freely. I believe that He is showing Himself strong through me, and He will do it through you too! Just say "Yes!"

> *Lord, you have called me to sow into your kingdom, to bear fruit, to share love. I am, without reservation, offering my loaves and fishes—do what you will. In Jesus' name, Amen.*

Drawn by Love

Day Six

Contributed by Sandra J. Courtney

"I have loved you with an everlasting love; I have drawn you with unfailing kindness."

—Jeremiah 31:3b

I didn't come from a Christian family. When I was fifteen-years-old, my parents split up and my siblings and I were torn apart, divided between the two. Life seemed harsh and uncertain, and I needed someone to lean on. I found that dating Joe was a great escape from the rigid, unrealistic expectations at home. Early in the relationship, Joe took me to meet his parents and siblings. The welcome from Joe's mom was simple but extraordinary. She loved and accepted me without hesitation in a way that was unfamiliar to me—but I knew she was real. Not once did she ever criticize me or say anything harsh. She treated me with patience, as if I were a daughter—one of *her* family.

Within that next year, I became pregnant. Joe and I decided to get married. While there were a few whispers about my choosing a "white dress," Joe's mom simply supported me and helped however she could. Without judgement, she kept loving me and reminding me that Jesus loved me too.

I gave birth to a beautiful baby girl three days before I turned seventeen. I had no idea how to be a mother, but I tried my best to do what I thought I should. I loved that little girl with all my heart. Following her birth, I experienced a very difficult time of depression. While I didn't have the strength to care about life, there remained a strong sense that I had to be there for her.

Alcohol became a big part of our lives then, and only got worse as time went on. Along with infidelity, it almost destroyed our marriage. We were two people living under one roof, but the love wasn't there. I knew my mother-in-law was praying for us and her little affirmations that I was doing a good job were flickers of hope along the way.

After the birth of my second child, a son, I became sick with mononucleosis. During this illness, I began to experience severe fear, anxiety, and panic attacks. The suffering continued for five painful years. When I couldn't even go outside beyond my own back yard without having a panic attack, I knew something had to change.

Joe had accepted the Lord in 1979. In 1982, I hit rock bottom. It was then that I gave my heart and life to the Lord. I had so much to learn and understand, but every day I would get up and ask the Lord to help me make it through the day without falling apart. Slowly, each day got a little easier. The Lord was taking me one step at a time. My mother-in-law was my cheerleader, my friend, and my protector.

God began to restore our marriage, giving us a new love for each other. He did what seemed impossible. The Lord Jesus has blessed me so much over the years, and I'm so dependent on Him. I know He will never leave me or forsake me. A scripture the Lord gave to me was John 14:27: *"Peace I leave with you; my peace I give you. I do not give to you as the world gives. Do not let your hearts be troubled and do not be afraid."*

There is nothing we go through in life that the Lord will not help us with. Joe and I just celebrated our fiftieth anniversary! Praise the Lord for His faithfulness. He loves and accepts me unconditionally. He is truly my Saviour. I am so thankful that He showed me His healing love through the sincere care of my mother-in-law, who prayed us both through to Kingdom victory.

Thank you, Lord, for the encouragers in my life. Sometimes their brief word, their smile, or their small gift has been just what I needed. I bless them today for coming alongside to strengthen my journey with you.

Extravagant Love
Day Seven

"Worthy is the Lamb, who was slain, to receive power and wealth and wisdom and strength and honor and glory and praise!"
—Revelation 5:12b

The scene of Mary's humble devotion to Jesus described in John 12:1–8 is one of the most beautiful in all of scripture. It was six days before Passover, and Jesus had come to Bethany, where Mary, Martha, and Lazarus lived, likely to the home of Simon the leper. The people were still celebrating the astounding miracle of Lazarus being raised from the dead. A dinner was being held, very likely to express gratitude to Jesus. Martha was serving in token of her great respect for her master, and Mary had her eyes fixed on Jesus, whom she loved. Lazarus reclined at the table with Jesus.

Heads turned and some quiet gasps were heard as Mary took a pint of pure spikenard, a fragrant and expensive perfume worth about a year's wages and poured it upon the feet of Jesus. (In Mark's and Matthew's records, we learn that this perfume had been carried in an alabaster jar.) The entire room was filled with the fragrance of the perfume. The aroma of spikenard was an indication that the very best had been offered. In the Song of Solomon, spikenard is mentioned as representing a passion or a deep love. Mary anointed His body as an act of devotion, believing in Him as the Messiah and the son of God. Only the best was worthy of her Lord, and she was willing to give it all.

As Mary poured out her extravagant worship, she wiped His feet with her hair. A woman's long hair was regarded as her glory. The washing of feet was a task reserved for a servant and not the members of the household, but Mary was humbly taking on a servant role as she worshipped Jesus.

Some of those present were indignant over Mary's act of worship. After all, the contents of the alabaster box could have been sold and given to the poor. They saw her worship as out of place, poorly timed, and wasteful. The objections of Judas, though sounding reasonable, were deceitfully motivated by his own disappointment that kept him concerned about selfish gain, not about caring for the poor. Jesus promptly addressed Judas's rebuke of Mary and instructed him to leave her alone. Matthew's and Mark's accounts add that Jesus called what Mary had done to Him "a beautiful thing."

I am reminded that we too can choose to worship Him in abandon, pouring our love on Him. Those moments alone with Jesus, with eyes fixed on Him, are sweet and powerful. But when others are nearby, we may find them offended and uncomfortable. I'm not talking *only* about Sunday mornings in church or at prayer meeting, although corporate worship is a wonderful opportunity! I'm talking about living out a lifestyle of worship in which we conduct our day as a sacrifice of worship to Him—when we worship with our work, our finances, our time, our attitudes. And when things go wrong, we still worship, because he is worthy. This kind of living releases a sweet aroma of Heaven into the atmosphere around us, as do our sacred and cherished moments alone with Him.

Consider taking some time today to break your alabaster box at his feet. Pour out some extravagant love on the one who is worthy of your best and then take that same love for Him and choose to live your life emitting a sweet fragrance that draws others to recognize His worthiness.

Jesus, I don't want to miss any moments of filling the atmosphere with my worship to you. I bow before you now, and I worship you. You are worthy. I give you honour and glory, praise and adoration. May my offering to you be a beautiful thing.

God's Court

Day Eight
Contributed by Crystal Barley

For his sake I have discarded everything else, counting it all as garbage, so that I could gain Christ... I no longer count on my own righteousness ... rather, I become righteous through faith in Christ.

—Philippians 3:8–9, NLT

Three years ago, we moved down South. You can't get further south than we are in Alabama. Here your tea is sweet, cornbread salty, God is first, and sports are life. If your kid can walk, then he can run, so let's put a basketball, bat, or football in those hands and get 'um out there!

Last year, my son's basketball team won the championship! My son hustled at every practice, was attentive to the coaches, and encouraged his teammates every game, all season. But ... he's a terrible basketball player. He runs like he's wading in waist deep water, shoots free throws like he's Ray Charles, and often forgets if he's playing defense or offense. I'm not sure how he would have managed without us yelling instructions from the bleachers. But, after each consistently won game, he would beam, full of pride, totally oblivious to his inadequacies.

When I rededicated my life to Christ at eighteen, I had Philippians 3:8–9 stamped into metal and wore it as a necklace to remind me that it wasn't my own works that would attract God's love. But it's hard to unwrite years of learned behaviours that were re-enforced with positive or negative actions by authority figures. Over time, I slowly fell back into a pattern of belief that, by my getting it right, I could earn God's favour and love.

I kept a mental tally sheet of what earned me my Christian badges and God's favour and love. I fasted once this week: one point; I gave financially to a missionary: five points. I didn't respond to a controversial Facebook post: twenty points. Then there were the subtraction points—yelled at my kids, binge-watched Netflix, cussed at the Subaru that cut me off. It was exhausting!

Last year my world came crashing down. Everything I tried to build and sustain began to teeter on the edge of ruins. I stood at the mercy of other people's life choices. My way of life, my job, my salary, and my family made a drastic shift. I was stripped of everything but God. I clung to Him … or He clung to me. I'm not sure which.

It was in that season of nothing that God became everything. It was never my works but my faith and faithfulness to God that found me favour. Everything else was garbage, as Paul says. I realized *He* had chosen *me!* As I've slowly rebuilt, God's love has been tangible, and His favour has embarrassed me. I've had to remind myself often that I am worthy of a good Father taking care of me.

Today I have a job that pays me to pursue my dream and education. Strangers and friends chose love, His love—they have given me financial gifts and emotional support by God's appointment. I've learned that I'm a lot like my son on that basketball court. I'm going to stumble, but it isn't my ability that earns the win—it's just me showing up, believing, every day on God's court. It's His win, His victory. C.S Lewis writes:

> (God) relies on the troughs even more than on the peaks; some of His special favorites have gone through longer and deeper troughs than anyone else … growing into the sort of creature He wants it to be … and if only the will to walk is really there He is pleased even with their stumbles."[1]

Jesus, righteous Lover of my soul. I declare today that I will show up each day, believing - knowing that your love will surround me, even in the stumbles.

---

1 "C.S. Lewis Quotes," *Goodreads*, accessed January 7, 2021, https://www.goodreads.com/quotes/8173537

The Imprint of Love

Day Nine

Contributed by Heather Bennett-Chamberlain

> "Therefore, as God's chosen people, holy and dearly loved, clothe yourselves with compassion, kindness, humility, gentleness and patience. Bear with each other and forgive one another if any of you has a grievance against someone. Forgive as the Lord forgave you. And over all these virtues put on love, which binds them all together in perfect unity."
>
> —Colossians 3:12–14

It's my favourite part of the house in which I grew up. Are you guessing the kitchen, where we gathered around the table as a family to eat and share about our days? Are you thinking it's my favourite chair, where I curled up reading *Little House on the Prairie*? If you know my home, a good guess would be that it was likely the beautiful front porch, where wild and wonderful water fights usually began. But no, it's the back step, the threshold I crossed for over forty years when returning home from school, from the park, from church, from a friend's. It's the step where I would sit when, occasionally, as a determined and annoyed little girl, I refused to finish my supper. It's the step where I had my first kiss. It's the step that led to a doorway to security and comfort, warmth, and family. But what was it that made this step so special to me?

The back step tells a story. You see, the house I grew up in is over 130 years old. The step is a four-inch slab of hardwood. What makes it special is how worn it has become over the years. One-hundred-and-thirty years of people stepping on it to cross the threshold has made its mark. Years of footprints going in and out have caused the centre of the step to be worn an inch and a half smaller than the remainder of the structure. Worn smooth.

Choosing Love

I got to thinking about that ... 130 years of people making an imprint on this house. One-hundred-and-thirty years of lives. Whether people lived here for forty-five years like my parents, coming and going daily, or just crossed the threshold once or more to visit. Each footprint has made its mark.

The way we lead our lives is similar. Each day we cross the threshold of other people's lives and leave a mark. We get to choose what kind of imprint we leave. Each day as we meet strangers, we can choose our response: Will I love them today? Will they matter? For that brief moment of time when we cross another's path, will our words and actions leave an imprint of love? We may feel that the little part we can play is insignificant, but moments of love build up over time and can soften even a calloused heart. Consistency in our love to the people around us can transform a life and bring value and acceptance—through us but sent from the Father.

Let us live our lives with compassion, kindness, and humility. Let's be patient with each other and those around us. Let us forgive and put on love. Matthew 25:40 says, *"And the King will answer them, 'Truly, I say to you, as you did it to one of the least of these my brothers, you did it to me'"* (ESV). May the love that God has so graciously, amazingly given us be the love that forever puts its imprint on someone's heart.

Jesus, set your burning love upon me once again this day. As I cross the threshold of other's lives, may my steps be marked with the things that matter to you— kindness, care, humility, patience, grace, and mercy. May my steps matter not just for today but for eternity.

"Not all of us can do great things. But we can do small things with great love."
—Mother Teresa

Loving God and Letting Go

Day Ten

> "Love the Lord your God with every passion of your heart, with all the energy of your being, and with every thought that is within you."
> —Matthew 22:37b, TPT

Paul says we are to *"throw off everything that hinders us and the sin that so easily entangles us"* (Hebrews 12:1). Hindrances can trip us up, slow us down, and keep us from being fully open to His love. Letting go on some days is a moment-by-moment practice. At other times, it's a life-altering decision in which God's love for us presents an opportunity for a new and better way.

A dear friend, Betty, has recounted to me a story of a time in her life as a new Christian when letting go saved her from a detour that could have meant missing her destiny. A musician with a #1 hit on the country music charts and a nomination for Top Female Performance/Country Music Artist of the Year, Betty describes it in her recently released book, *Out of the Flame*:

> I found myself with two feet firmly planted in Christ, but with a little toe that had gotten stuck on a fence. We had invested $7,000 in a new secular recording with songs that I had written … which… were about to catch fire … all the finances, time, and effort we'd taken would be wasted if I decided to "go gospel." … the release was scheduled in less than a week. I was ambivalent … drawn to the … sincerity with which he (the Apostle Paul) expressed his love … to Christ … however, too blinded by the

picture of fame and fortune to even consider what I had to gain by obedience.[2]

For Paul, to truly know Him meant letting go of everything from his past. (Philippians 3:7–8). Betty wrestled it out with God and knew He was telling her to let the promise of fame and the lucrative contract go. When her decision was made, God's love was outpoured to her with fresh inspiration for new songs, all expressing His divine nature, His unlimited love, and His incredible joy. He set her on a pathway of international, national, and local ministry in which her music and testimony has brought hundreds to Christ. As Betty says, "Praise God, that little toe was no longer stuck on the fence, and I was walking unrestricted on the path He had ordained for me."[3]

Her story reminds me of the rich young ruler who approached Jesus asking what he would need to do to gain eternal life. God saw his heart and knew what would prevent him from grasping the full measure of His love—it was his possessions. Jesus looked at him and loved him. He extended to this man a radical invitation to let go. The thought of such a sacrifice left the man grieving and sad. He could not see what he had to gain.

Letting go of anything and surrendering to God means, "Not my will but yours. I will walk in obedience to your plan for me." Jesus showed us this in the garden when He agonized over His trip to the cross. He had to let go of desiring a different way. It was painful, yet He trusted His Father and surrendered. In the same way, we must hear and obey in both the small and big things where God, in ultimate love for us, is saying, "Let it go."

Jesus, I know I need to be fully committed to your work in my life. What am I hanging on to that's holding me back from my true destiny in you?

---

2   Betty Chisholm, *Out of the Flame* (Winnipeg: Word Alive Press, 2019), 136–137.
3   Ibid., 139.

Will You Be a Neighbour?

Day Eleven

"Love the Lord your God with all your heart ... soul ... strength and ... mind and, 'Love your neighbor as yourself.'"

—Luke 10:27

Fred Rogers, popularly known as "Mister Rogers" from his famed children's show, *Mr. Rogers' Neighborhood*, passed away in 2003, one month before his seventy-fifth birthday. Mr. Rogers, a favourite in our house, hosted one of the longest-running shows in the history of PBS. The 2019 film *A Beautiful Day in the Neighborhood* tells his story. Fred Rogers was not only an American television host and producer but a Presbyterian minister who saw his show as a ministry tool. Each show he posed the same question: "Won't you be my neighbour?"

Luke 10 records the words of the law as quoted by an expert in the law who had just asked Jesus what he must do to inherit eternal life. To justify and vindicate himself, and to trap Jesus, he demanded clarification on who might be considered a neighbour. In Jesus' reply, we are treated to one of the world's most superb short stories: the story of the Good Samaritan. A man going from Jerusalem to Jericho was attacked by robbers along the way, who left him badly beaten and stripped of his clothes. Three different travellers came upon this helpless victim, and each had his own response. The priest crossed to the other side of the road, relinquishing any responsibility to help. The Levite counted the risk and did the same. But the Samaritan (viewed by Jews as inferior and even repulsive) immediately felt compassion for the man, bandaged his wounds, and took him to a nearby inn, paying for his care and recovery.

Jesus asked the lawyer which one of these he would consider a neighbour. The "clever" lawyer was cornered—he had to choose the one who had shown compassion. Jesus then directed him to go and do the same.

Consider a few of the many lessons about love that Jesus taught in this story. There will be times when we must be willing to leave our personal comfort zones in order to show love. The Samaritan was a traveller too, and he had somewhere he needed to be, but he was willing to rearrange his priorities to attend to the wounded man. Mother Teresa once said:

> The biggest disease today is not leprosy or cancer or tuberculosis, but rather the feeling of being unwanted, uncared for, deserted by everybody. The greatest evil is the lack of love and charity, the terrible indifference towards one's neighbor who lives at the roadside, the victim of exploitation, corruption, poverty, and disease.[4]

God loves us, and His life-giving love enables us to love others into wholeness and freedom. We can't offer the type of love God desires without the strength of the Holy Spirit. It's not simply a feeling but a choice, and it matters that the love becomes an action. We're not meant to act "as if" we love someone, but we are to act *because* we love them. We instinctively tend to limit the possibilities for whom we exert ourselves, but Jesus has shown us here that anyone in need is our neighbour. What in your life shows that you are in love with God? Which "neighbour" is Jesus asking you to love today through the power of His Spirit?

Jesus, I'm done with limiting you by choosing who will be my neighbour. Take my repentant heart and let it beat with a new rhythm that transforms my convictions into actions of love.

---

[4] "Quote of the Day," *Idlehearts*, https://www.idlehearts.com/1202123/, accessed February 12, 2021.

When You Long for One More Gift

Day Twelve

Contributed by Shelly Calcagno

"Thanks be to God for his indescribable gift."

—2 Corinthians 9:15

I remember the year when I was finally the same shoe size as my mom. I was likely around fourteen, and I had waited years it seemed to catch up to her size eight. When I finally hit that number, I felt like I had arrived (mostly because my shoe wardrobe doubled!) From then on, my sweet mom would always share her shoes.

It didn't stop there.

She actually shared everything she had with me. Always. She'd give me the clothes off her back, pulled out from her closet, or something from a shopping bag she'd just bought for herself. Things from the cupboards, storage, boxes, totes—almost anything you could imagine.

"You can have this," she'd say. Just one of the million ways she would show her love to me. She loved Jesus too, and I always felt like everything she did reflected His love that shone through her life.

And now so many things have changed. Love expressed in this time of life is different. We've been walking the longest goodbye journey with her as Alzheimer's takes more and more away. But there are still gifts of love in the middle of it all. Sometimes it's the recognition in her face when I sit beside her, or the slip of my name when I least expect it, holding hands walking through the house, or quiet moments together watching a movie. I treasure all these times, but I miss sharing things with my mom. I miss her gifts. Not because I care about things, but because I knew it meant she was thinking about me. It was one of the ways she showed her love.

Sometimes I wished I could have one more gift. Awhile back my dad told me to look in their front closet, because there were things she wasn't using anymore. I don't like to take any of her belongings, because she is still here, and my heart wants her to need them. But when I looked in the closet, I saw some boots. Beautiful, lovely black boots that she won't be wearing again. And I had just said I needed new boots. Mine, as per the story of my footwear life, were falling apart. "Take them," my dad said. So I did, and when I got home and put them in my closet, I remembered what my heart had been longing for.

One more gift.

I've worn those boots almost every day since, and I realize they represent other things in my life too: how I'm taking giant steps of bravery every week into a great unknown, making decisions, and trying to navigate middle-age life. Every day is made up of a million little steps, and most of the time they feel scary and uncertain.

But I keep walking. I don't have to be afraid of what's ahead, because He's right there walking with me. Each step I take, His presence is in my life. The little girl who couldn't wait to catch up and wear her sweet mama's shoes? Well, now I'm hoping the steps I take are ones worth following too. I'm following God in my journey, and all that she has given me is part of each step too.

The longest goodbye is a hard path to take. But I'm finding beauty along the way.

Each step.

Led by God. Inspired by my mom.

I'm thankful for all the gifts. For love, and presence, and never walking alone.

Jesus, some of the pathways on our journey together are really hard. In those painful parts, help me to remember that you are still walking with me. Thank you for the reflections of your love that assure me you are here.

A Labour of Love
Day Thirteen

The Lord appeared... saying, "I have loved you with an everlasting love; Therefore I have drawn you with kindness."

—Jeremiah 31:3 NASB

His father, Isaac, had blessed him and sent him off to Haran to find a wife. Armed with the precious promise of God's presence, Jacob headed for Haran, the land of his mother's family. It was a long and lonely journey, but ordered steps brought him to a field in Haran where his uncle's flocks were to be watered. When he arrived at the well that day, he was captivated by a young woman, the daughter of this Uncle Laban—it was love at first sight. As the sheep lapped up the water he had drawn, his eyes remain focussed on this angelic young lady. His heart pounding, he leaned in and gently kissed her. As he did, he began to weep aloud. For Jacob, this wasn't just a passing fancy while on his quest—there was a spiritual conviction and a confidence that this one would be his bride. His sense of certainty was confirmed as her father, Laban, invited him in to stay.

Jacob's love for Rachel had grown like a well-fed fire. He hesitated as he considered the desire of his heart and the potential for its realization. Rachel was beyond beautiful. She had an older sister, Leah, who was tender-eyed and available, but Jacob wasn't moved toward her. Rachel had won his heart, and he needed to speak with her father.

Jacob and Laban agreed that Jacob would serve for seven years so that he might take Rachel as his wife. Seven years for most searching young men would be more than they could bear, but *love partnered with patience*, and those seven years seemed to Jacob like only a few days.

Laban marked the calendar, and when the seven years had passed, he gathered together the whole community and made a great wedding feast. Awakening the morning after the wedding, Jacob realized that he was the victim of Laban's deceit. He had spent his wedding night with Rachel's sister, Leah, and his heart was broken. Devastated and outraged, he confronted Laban. Laban insisted that he stay with Leah for the full week of her marital festivities and then he could have Rachel. The new price? Another seven years. Jacob's response unveils a true steadfast, sacrificial love for Rachel. He would press past the betrayal and deception, not only for himself, but for the sake of the one he loved. This is the deepest, purest kind of love—no labour was too hard to endure. Another seven years wouldn't stop Jacob. Patience and deep love would woo them both to realize the desire of their hearts and keep them steadfast as the debt was being paid.

God was with Jacob and He didn't abandon him during the challenging and often troubled journey that followed. Love has the potential to make the hard things in life more bearable, as it did for Jacob.

When life is unfair, unyielding, or disappointing, and things don't go as planned, there's a beautiful peace and security in knowing that God is still working on our behalf. There's strength and comfort in remembering that through His death and resurrection, Jesus purchased us so that we might be His special treasure and unique possession. The Great Lover of the universe is in love with us, always and forever. He will lavish His love, provision, protection, and grace upon us, and that love can make everything more bearable. We can choose His love right now and enjoy it for an uninterrupted eternity. (I John 4:19)

> *Lord, I love how you love me. I will not forget what Jesus did so that I could be reconciled with you eternally. Your love makes everything more bearable, and it brings me joy even in the challenges. Keep me steadfast as I walk in you.*

Love Stirs the Nest
Day Fourteen

"Be devoted to tenderly loving your fellow believers as members of one family. Try to outdo yourselves in respect and honor of one another."
—Romans 12:10, TPT

In the ways of an eagle, you will find a remarkable depiction of those who have a desire to soar. As ones who are called and chosen by the Lord, we are meant to exhibit many of the distinctive traits of an eagle such as learning how to know when it's time to take flight, obtain strength for the journey, gain altitude, rise above the storms, have keen vision, and practise endurance.

I was blessed to run with an eagle, a spiritual mentor/mother who had a vision for my life that was beyond what I could see. I met Barbara when my children were preteens. I had to cross into the US to meet with her, but her tenacity, confidence, and commitment to grow me were nothing short of an overwhelming *gift of love*. Vision for the future is constantly before those who are God's eagles, and they never settle for simply maintaining the present. Sometimes the future seems more realistic to them than the present. Such was the case for Barb—she saw, prophetically, a picture of my life before I even knew what that meant.

Eagles of God dream big dreams. They can believe for things that others, whose eyes are riveted to things of earth, cannot conceive. They understand that true vision is about the desires God imparts to us. Barb taught me how to be uncomfortable and hungry when I wasn't manifesting my full purpose, and she did this like an eagle.

When a mother eagle builds her nest, she starts with thorns, broken branches, sharp rocks, and a number of other items that seem entirely unsuitable for the project. But then she lines the nest with a thick padding of wool, feathers, and animal furs, making it soft and comfortable for the eggs. By the time the growing birds reach flying age, the comfort of the nest makes them quite reluctant to transition. That's when the mother eagle begins "stirring up the nest" so that the eaglets will be forced to fly (Deuteronomy 32:11).

As I observed Barb in her coaching sessions with others, her healing prayer ministry, and her women's ministry meetings, I saw her share her skills, her rich anointing, and her passion to see others made whole. Occasionally she'd find reasons to have to "leave" a session, and she'd ask a hesitant and terrified me to finish. She was stirring the nest, getting me ready to fly.

In all of this, I learned Paul's principle and exhortation to "... *imitate my walk with God...*" (Philippians 3:17 TPT). Often I was frustrated and even angry that Barb had left me holding the bag, or given me an "impromptu" ministry opportunity that scared me half to death ... not realizing until later she was just "stirring the nest." Only love can give people like Barb the heart to take such a risk. She was teaching me to dwell in His presence and draw on the anointing of His Spirit.

This journey of personal and spiritual growth is a story of *selfless love* that was part of equipping me for my purpose. Perhaps you haven't found a "mama eagle" yet to help you along; nevertheless, the Lord may be getting ready to push you off to heights that you've never dreamed of. Don't be fearful: "*He will cover you with his feathers. He will shelter you with his wings*" (Psalm 91:4). Have you been wondering why you are restless, or doubting that you're even in the will of God? Doubt no longer—it's not the wrath of God trying to destroy you, it is the *love of God* making you willing to take flight into the next part of the plan that He has for you. I dare you to take the challenge and enjoy the new adventure.

> *Go ahead, Father, I get it! You are stirring the nest because you love me. I align my heart with your purpose for my life, and I trust in your undergirding love to get me there.*

Living Out an Endless Love
Day Fifteen

"...and walk in the way of love, just as Christ loved us and gave himself up for us as a fragrant offering and sacrifice to God."
—Ephesians 5:2

Grandma Dinnick lived in a quaint little white cottage in Orangeville, Canada. Her door was never locked, her dining room table was regularly set for extras, and her heart was always overflowing with genuine love and generosity. Grandma Dinnick knew how to live out the love of Jesus. She opened the big family Bible, read aloud, and prayed each day between 9:00 a.m. and 10:00 a.m.—nothing took precedence over her daily appointment with God!

Having had the opportunity to stay with Grandma Dinnick during some of my early teen years, I was blessed to see the love she shared in so many practical ways. She had lovingly adopted a fragile and underweight infant who wasn't expected to do well. I just knew her as Aunt Marion, sister to my mom, and a fully fledged part of the family. An elderly church member, Velma, whose family was on the mission field, was given the "front bedroom," where she remained comfortable and cared for until she left for Heaven. Grandma's couch was always available for me for a time of "retreat" from my three conniving and adventurous brothers. It could be for three hours or three months—it never mattered to Grandma. Leftovers from meals were always placed in a basket, covered with a linen cloth and carried by one of us to the Pike family a few doors down. Extended family and friends were given a haven for healing in her "back bedroom" for as long as they needed.

I remember her often quoting from one of her favourite songs while engaged in household chores.

> *Could we with ink the ocean fill,*
> *And were the skies of parchment made;*
> *Were ev'ry stalk on earth a quill,*
> *And ev'ry man a scribe by trade;*
> *To write the love of God above*
> *Would drain the ocean dry;*
> *Nor could the scroll contain the whole*
> *Tho' stretched from sky to sky.*[5]

This third verse of "The Love of God is Greater Far" is a translation of an Aramaic poem written in 1050 A.D. by a Jewish poet.

> We can imagine this poet standing on the shores of the Mediterranean Sea, contemplating the great love of his Jehovah ... As the love of God sweeps over ... his ... soul, his imagination fills the ocean with ink, the arching skies seem to magnify the scope of this all-compelling love, and the papyrus marsh comes to life with countless scribes writing ceaselessly and tirelessly about the measureless love of God.[6]

With that backdrop, I appreciate even more these words by which Grandma would remind herself and others just how much God loves us. Had she also pictured the scene? Perhaps... but I know that Grandma was convinced of His love in the depths of her spirit, and it compelled her to love without limit everyone God sent her way. Clearly, when one begins to grasp the expanse of God's love, one can live out that love toward others in a selfless and beautiful abandon.

---

5   "The Love of God," Stanza Three, *Hymnary.org*, accessed November 12, 2020, https://hymnary.org/text/the_love_of_god_is_greater_far

6   "Music of the Message: The Story of 'The Love of God,'" *Ministry International*, accessed on November 12, 2020, https://www.ministrymagazine.org/archive/1950/09/the-story-of-the-love-of-god

Lord, your love is boundless, deep, and overflowing. Thank you for your many expressions of love in my life. Teach me to love without limits. In Jesus' name, Amen.

The Power of His Love

Day Sixteen

"... perfect love expels all fear. If we are afraid ... this shows that we have not fully experienced his perfect love."

—1 John 4:18, NLT

Today's highlighted verse is from the book of 1 John, where John the apostle is teaching us how to live like Jesus. He emphasizes that living like Jesus results from abiding in Him and that we have been empowered to overcome through the anointing of the Holy Spirit. We also learn about the lavish love of the Father—a rich, pure, powerful love that expels fear.

While giving oversight to many prayer coaching and healing sessions, I've become aware of the deficit of love when people of God are bound by fear. Some of the common areas we often address are: fear of failure, fear of intimacy, fear of the future, fear of man, fear of rejection, and fear of being alone. Though small worries aren't great fears, living with a stream of small worries opens the door to fear. We can feed thoughts and concerns that were never meant to grow. Sometimes, because of wounding, it becomes difficult to receive the love of another without being suspicious of their motives or fearing being let down. Sometimes, contrary to God's Word, we just choose to live in the "what ifs" instead of the present.

To the "what if" worriers, Corrie Ten Boom says, "Worry does not empty tomorrow of its sorrow. It empties today of its strength."[7] In situations of wounding, embracing the truth of God's love for us may feel like a

---

[7] "Corrie Ten Boom Quotes," *BrainyQuote*, accessed February 12, 2021, https://www.brainyquote.com/quotes/corrie_ten_boom_135203

risk. It's sometimes hard to see beyond those past hurts and allow ourselves to try again. That's why this particular scripture is a game changer. Perfect love casts out fear. We can't just wish it away. We have the authority in Christ to break the power of that spirit of fear. Invite His perfect love to take its place. Demolishing the old habits and patterns of thinking and acting requires patience and perseverance—it's a process. Forgiveness is a key—receiving God's forgiveness and releasing forgiveness toward those who have wounded us and brought fear into our lives. Sometimes there's also a need to forgive ourselves.

One of my all-time favourite healing and wholeness teachers, Jack Frost, says this:

> It is in the Sea of Fear that we make our choices to break free of the entanglements of life ... It is in the Sea of Fear that our pain begins to outweigh our shame and we seek the change that will lead us into the fulfilment of our purpose for life. It is in the Sea of Fear that we discover the hindrances that have almost drowned many of us. It is in the midst of the greatest fear ... that we ... are faced with the decision to "Live, Live, Live."[8]

When we're able to come free of the fear and receive God's perfect love and His acceptance, we'll understand our significance and begin to live as a "loved one." It's so worth it!

Is it time to break free from fear and walk in His life-giving love? Are you willing to trust in the power of His Holy Spirit to set you free? The Lord wants to give you His unchanging, unending, and unrestricted love. You can learn to trust Him and His plan for your life so that you can once again take the risk of loving and being loved. May you be stirred by His Spirit today to say yes to His warm embrace and powerful love.

> *Loving Father, I invite you, by your Spirit, to search the hidden places in my heart that have been harbouring fears. I choose to trust the safety of your embrace. I declare today in my life that your love wins!*

---

[8] Jack and Trisha Frost, *Unbound* (Shippensburg, PA: Destiny Image Publishers, 2012), 44–45.

Lost and Alone and Longing for Love

Day Seventeen

Contributed by Laurie Florek

"Do not say, "I will repay evil"; Wait [expectantly] for the Lord, and He will rescue and save you."

—Proverbs 20:22, AMP

My heart is always stirred with testimonies of the loving Heavenly Father who has rescued people in difficult situations. For a good part of my life, I could only long to be rescued—by someone. My home broke up when I was five, and my sister and I weren't re-united with our mother until I was thirteen. After years of living as invisible and rejected, the reunion was welcomed and comforting—briefly.

One morning, without warning, two police officers banged at the door to take us to court. To say I was in a daze would be an understatement. I found myself standing anxiously before a judge who called my sister and I "incorrigible." What did that mean? We were remanded and placed in custody for seven days for assessment. The "observation home" to which we were assigned was temporarily closed, so we were housed in Barton Street Jail—161 hours that no thirteen-year-old should ever have to go through.

In court the following week (August 1, 1955), the judge called my mother unfit. My heart broke, and I swore at him expressively. The outburst netted me three years in Galt Reform School, the worst of the worst. My attempt to run meant thirty days in solitary detention. Emptiness. No bed, no bathroom (just a pot), no clothes (yes, naked). Food came once a day and a shower once week. An additional solitary was incurred for a second running attempt and stealing a toothbrush—this time for sixty days, which ended with a nervous breakdown. These revolting three years set me on a path of pain and hopelessness. I was robbed of days that might have been beautiful, filled with joy and new adventures.

When I moved to Grimsby as a wounded and hardened attempted suicide survivor in 2001, everything changed! My new hairdresser, Pat, seemed very different. Being an atheist, I was shocked that she had me thinking about God. I told Pat that I felt sorry for her choosing to believe—she was so duped!

She invited me to join her in a Bible study she was starting. I liked Pat, so I joined simply to do my part in helping her group understand there was no God. Weeks later, bathed in the love of that group, there was an awakening in my soul. In the privacy of my own home, I said the salvation prayer and started drinking all I could get of the love of Jesus. There was a lot of time to make up for!

I now know the truth that He knew me before I was born, He loved me, and He has never left me. He has used what the enemy meant for harm to make something good of my life. I have chosen to leave the questions with Him. I have many health issues with "tentative" prognoses, and every new day is a gift from Him.

> Though we are incomplete, God loves us completely. Though we are imperfect, He loves us perfectly. Though we may feel lost and without compass, God's love encompasses us completely... He loves every one of us, even those who are flawed, rejected, awkward ... or broken."[9]

His love has changed my life, and that same love is available to you. You can't go back and change the beginning, but you can start where you are and change the ending.[10]

> *Jesus, testimonies of your transformation in others reminds me that you are well able to handle my requests today. Let me be contented in the power of your love. Amen.*

---

9 "60 Inspirational Quotes about God's Love," *Inspiring Tips*, accessed February 12, 2021, https://inspiringtips.com/quotes-about-god-love/

10 "C.S. Lewis Quotes," *Quotefancy*, accessed December 30, 2020, https://quotefancy.com/clive-staples-lewis-quotes

The Sacrifice of Love
Day Eighteen

"And walk in love, as Christ loved us and gave himself up for us, a fragrant offering and sacrifice to God."

—Ephesians 5:2, ESV

When we begin to follow Christ, we resolve to love God even if it costs us. It can cost us a variety of things, from our pride, our comfort, our preferences, our time, our financial resources, and our entitlement to things like convenience and popularity. When we resolve to love God and obey His commands, He might require of us some things we didn't expect.

Consider Abraham. After twenty-five years of expectation, waiting, wanting, and wondering, the child of promise is born. How much Isaac would have meant to both Sarah and Abraham! Then God instructs Abraham: *"Take your son, your only son, whom you love—Isaac—and go to the region of Moriah. Sacrifice him there as a burnt offering on a mountain I will show you"* (Genesis 22:2).

Abraham had loved God for a long time, and he trusted Him. As he took that two-day journey to the mountain, he did it with full commitment to obey while not having the answers to what must have been some burning questions. We know the end of the story. God provided a sacrificial ram and spared Isaac. God was after Abraham's heart, not his son. But Abraham proved his total love for God in his willingness to sacrifice even the son for whom he had waited for years.

In 2 Samuel, David built an altar to the Lord on Araunah's threshing floor. Araunah saw that David would need not only the threshing floor but an offering to give, so he offered David oxen, threshing sledges, and anything else he required. I love David's response to Araunah: *"No, I insist on paying you for it. I will not sacrifice to the Lord my God burnt offerings that cost me nothing"* (2 Samuel 24:24). Any sacrifice that speaks love must come from the heart ... and there will be a cost.

Our heart is often the sacrifice that most pleases Him. *"My sacrifice, O God, is a broken spirit; a broken and contrite heart you, God, will not despise"* (Psalm 51:17). Outward actions alone, no matter how good they are, are not a gift of love to the Father if our heart isn't in it.

Sometimes we know God is asking us to show our love for Him through specific decisions or actions, but it's a struggle! Looking back, I realize how often sacrifices of love were made by my parents for my brothers and me. I wish I had appreciated those more at the time. Their generation, because of war, restriction, and rationing, was familiar with sacrifice. Many of their friends and family sacrificed their lives for the love of country, family, friends, and their futures.

Sacrifice is the essence of godly love. It's as plain as that. Sacrifice was a way of life with Jesus, and it's to become our way of life and our way of love in our interactions with one another. As it does, we become the living sacrifices we are called to be in Romans 12:1: *"Take your every day, ordinary life—your sleeping, eating, going-to-work, and walking-around life—and place it before God as an offering"* (MSG). That's the call to sacrificial love, and that's where it begins—on the altar.

Jesus, today you have reminded me that love must come from the heart. I am so prone to put my own interests first. I offer you my heart—all of who you have made me to be. The cost cannot compare with all you have done for me.

As a Mother Loves Her Children

Day Nineteen

Contributed by Jenna Harmon

"... I have loved you with an everlasting love ..."

—Jeremiah 31:3

Motherhood didn't come quite as naturally to me as I thought it would. I always knew I wanted to be a mom, but my experience with my first was challenging. I was overwhelmed with how many things didn't "come naturally," even though I had cherished my dolls, babysat a ton, and came fully equipped with child-bearing hips! The love I have for him grew over time because we went through hard things. We overcame together. He needed me, and I rose to the challenge. Then, all of a sudden, we were expecting number two, and I didn't know if I could possibly love anyone else quite as much as I loved the first. I cried so many tears during that second pregnancy, wondering if I'd be enough for both of them. After all, he had made me into a mother, softening my edges in ways our marriage never could.

Our second arrived and I got to relish in every moment. All of the stages I'd wished away with my eldest suddenly felt like sand between my fingers, and I begged time to slow down. I hoped he'd fall asleep in my arms instead of putting him down at every opportunity so I could "get things done." What things? What's more important than these two precious gifts from the Lord? It's true—"Motherhood is a million little moments that God weaves together with grace, redemption, laughter, tears, and most of all, love."[11]

---

[11] Lysa TerKeurst, "15 Beautiful Quotes about Christian Mothers," *Christ-Centered Mama*, accessed February 12, 2021, https://christcenteredmama.com/15-beautiful-christian-mothers-day-card-quotes/

These boys of mine, forever longed for but not mine forever. Just for now. They were God's plan for these million little moments.

Just for a little while. What am I doing with that time? You know, besides kissing boo boos, making meals, and convincing them to go to sleep. All is not perfect, and I have to pray for added strength most days … for patience, gentleness, and all the rest. Yes, the early years can seem slow and full of what feels mundane or routine. But their eyes are watching me, and little ears are listening too. Listening to my prayers, feeling the weight of my discipline in love, watching how Mommy and Daddy speak to one another. What a thing it is to hold your dreams in your arms and kiss them goodnight. I recognize the gifts that I have been entrusted with for a season and am so grateful God gave them to me.

As it turns out, I discovered that the love comes *with the child*. My love really was enough for *both* of them at the *same* time. Motherhood has given me a glimpse into understanding the love God has for me while loving seven billion other people at the same time. It's a different love with each child—unique, personal, and attentive. His care and concern are no less with each one. Matthew 10:29–31 says that He knows everything about us, including the number of hairs on our head. In that total love of our God is not just an awareness but an equal, consistent love. He loves us just the same. I understand that verse so much better now.

"As a mother loves her children" is more than a poetic cliché. I'm learning so much about how He loves me and loves *through me*. Thank you, God, for my two precious children—true gifts from you. No, I can't hold back the hands of the clock, and I wouldn't hurry time along! But I can hold their hands with a confidence that these many moments of love are shaping their lives and ours as well!

> *God, your love is so vast and yet so personal. As I receive your love today, help me to consistently and generously share that love with those in my sphere of influence, so that they too may experience your presence and your care.*

Refreshing Love
Day Twenty

The Lord your God in your midst, The Mighty One, will save; He will rejoice over you with gladness, He will quiet you with His love . . .
—Zephaniah 3:17, NKJV

As women with job descriptions as broad as the ocean and with packed schedules, we're sometimes desperately lacking in our ability to find time alone with God. Though the longing for moments to be refreshed in His love may be deep in our hearts, we tend to spend time meeting the needs of others, and time alone with God often takes a back seat. We have an awareness, however, that we can't be to our family, our employers, or our community what we hope to be unless we have deeper personal fellowship with God and not just a surface relationship.

As we invest personal time to receive His love, our capacity to love others increases. Our hearts need to be refilled with the revelation that God accepts us, deeply loves us, values us, and cheers us on. The scripture says that nothing we ever do or fail to do will keep us from His love. (Romans 8:38). On some days, the best we can manage is "Jesus, I know you're here. Help me make it through this day." For this, He will never condemn us, for His love is limitless. He sees our need and comes to fill us.

He works in our emptiness. Like the vessels of the widow at Zarephath by the dried-up brook (1 Kings 17), and the prophet's wife with only a little oil left (2 Kings 4), when there is no more need, no emptiness, the pouring stops. He's familiar with empty vessels—those who find themselves depleted but are humble and thirsty for His love and refreshing. I think perhaps He even prefers to use the cracked and dry most often, as we're more likely to leak His love to those around us.

Sometimes we can even find ourselves in a wilderness. We're not sure what detour we took to get there, and we're not sure what to do next. In those seasons, we can feel very alone facing discouragement and even hopelessness, with seemingly no way to turn things around. Sometimes it's an accumulation of circumstances that are out of our control. Of course, there are times when we are physically weary and need others to lend a hand, but when our soul is worn out, we need moments with Him to be refilled.

Hagar stands out as a unique Bible personality—the surrogate mother for Sarah and Abraham, since Sarah struggled with infertility. Hagar didn't choose motherhood, but she did choose to make things worse by mocking Sarah's childlessness. Sarah responded by humiliating and mistreating Hagar, forcing her to run away into a wilderness. She didn't plan that time alone, but she got there out of desperation. Apart from the conflict and quarrels, God spoke to Hagar near a spring in the desert and told her what to do (Genesis 16:9–13). He reminded her that He saw her and knew her, and He revealed a picture of His plan for her future. He quieted her with His love. For Hagar to make her way out of that wilderness took a lot of trust and a good helping of God's grace. Hagar used her wilderness to listen and gain strength, and God met her there.

While the many expectations can be exhausting, God's love can bring restoration, strength, and an ability to love like Jesus. He will strengthen you to live amid circumstances that you can't change. He will quiet you with His love. If you need Him, just whisper that need to Him. He has promised that those who refresh others will themselves be refreshed by His limitless love.

> *Quiet me today, Father, and fill me afresh. I feel overtaxed and exhausted with (_____) (add your personal words here—the family, my job, the caregiving, the debts, etc.). I confess my emptiness and open myself to your refilling and refreshing.*

Love Unsolicited

Day Twenty-One

"Do not remember the former things ... I am about to do a new thing, Now it will spring forth.... I will even put ... Rivers in the desert."
—Isaiah 43:18–19 AMP

She was never named, this woman who lived in a society where women were disregarded, who belonged to a race despised by the Jews, and who lived in shame due to her choices in life. Though blemished with an unsavoury past, she had a heart that was open to life-changing revelation. Her encounter with Jesus at the well at Sychar in Samaria highlights for us the heart of Jesus—to give love, unsolicited, to a woman who had been "loved" by many men. He knew everything about her yet saw beyond her flaws (John 4:4–42).

Jesus was travelling through Samaria on the way to Galilee. Around noon, He encountered this woman of Samaria. She was coming to draw water from the well in Sychar. Jesus, thirsty and tired, sat down by the well. Her questions to Jesus were stark and pointed, and His responses were equally specific. Jesus asked for a drink, but knowing He was clearly a Jew, she asked how he could bring Himself to do this. His response was mystifying (v. 10). To a woman who spent part of each day hauling clay jugs to and from a well, water was a powerful symbol. When Jesus offered "living water" that would never run dry, she paid attention. The woman pressed him, *"Sir, give me this water so that I won't get thirsty and have to keep coming here to draw water"* (v. 15).

And then He draws back the curtain on her secret life to help her see that her soul hunger will never be satisfied physically. He exposed her sin not to shame her with it but to free her from it. He asked her to go and call her husband and come back, but she replied that she had no husband. That's when Jesus announced to her that she'd had five husbands, and the man she was now with was not her husband. (vv. 17–18). The woman, in awe, recognizes that this is no ordinary Jew. Her eyes were opening to the truth of who He was—Jesus, the Messiah, the anointed king who had come to seek and save the lost.

Instead of shame, spiritual refreshment flooded her soul. He was offering her forgiveness and access to His living water that would bring her eternal life. *She left her jug* and hurried to tell the townspeople what had happened. They were convinced—she had a testimony that could not be questioned, a witness to powerful supernatural love and redemption.

In leaving her water jug (vv. 28–30) to return to the people, she symbolically left behind the things she had looked to for value and identity in the past, the ways she'd tried to satisfy her soul. Now she had found living water, and she would not thirst again! When we experience His life-changing goodness, we will gratefully leave aside some things that have been our source of identity and limited fulfilment.

Like the woman at the well, we are often blind to our own need until we get a revelation of the anointed one. Jesus is the living water we need. When we put our faith and trust in Him, we will find an unending source of love, truth, and hope, and we can leave our false sense of satisfaction behind. Jesus sees our hearts. He sees our selfish choices, our weaknesses, and our secrets, yet He pursues us and loves us. When Jesus becomes our source of life, we will discover that His love is the greatest thing that has ever happened to us.

Jesus, I want to be one who leaves my water jug at the well. I want to be one who encounters you, talks with you, listens to you, and tells others that your love is deep, strong, and life-changing. The beauty of your redemptive love, O Lord, is that there is enough for all of us! Amen.

Love's Surprise

Day Twenty-Two
Contributed by Sulojana Sam

"...If you then, being evil, know how to give good gifts to your children, how much more will your Father who is in heaven give good things to those who ask Him!"

—Matthew 7:11, NKJV (emphasis added)

One wintry evening in November 2015, just before we sat down to pray together, my husband, Jeeva, and I went over the prayer targets we'd be focusing on for our prayer time together. There was a new one that night, which shook me up momentarily—more than a little. "We're behind on our property taxes and need $10,000 plus by the end of December to pay it off."

My first thought was, *This is impossible!* But I didn't say it out aloud. I wanted to be wise to speak in faith and with confidence in who He is. We had seen His love poured out in many ways in times past, but this need would definitely require a miracle. I also knew that God is always looking for the open door to provide His blessings, and we can open that door through prayer.

We had just attended a conference a few days prior to that where we had received some fresh insight on how to pull down blessings from Heaven. Jeeva and I held hands together and came into agreement that God would meet this need. Then we raised our hands up into the "heavenly realm" and, in a prophetic act of faith, pulled down that exact amount from heaven.

In the following days, we kept thanking God for answering this prayer (1 Thessalonians 5:18). Nothing was changing in the bank account, and the time was drawing closer, but I had a supernatural peace of mind.

About a week later, I received a letter from The Public Employees Pension Plan (PEPP) in Saskatchewan: "Dear Sulojana Sam, PEPP has been searching for you. You have a pension benefit waiting in PEPP." I had worked for the Government of Saskatchewan when we'd lived there fifteen years earlier. Why would they be looking for me now? As I read on, the letter explained, "We are looking forward to reconnecting you and your pension."

Balancing somewhere between expectation and curiosity, I called their office. After scrutiny of my identity, they declared that I was the one they had been "searching for." There was a sum of pension money belonging to me that had been collecting interest for fifteen years! I would simply have to fill out a form to access the funds. Of course, I still had no idea how much money was involved.

After the representative had finished explaining everything, she finally revealed the amount. Undone, I wrote it down. There was a silence. I was overwhelmed. Speechless! Tears ran down my cheeks as I truly felt the extravagant love of my heavenly Father! It was the exact amount we needed to meet the deadline to pay off our property taxes! Jeeva and I were so thrilled! God had answered our prayers!

I got on my knees and thanked God for His love and provision. As Andrew Murray has said, "Answered prayer is the interchange of love between the Father and His child."[12] I encourage you to invite Him to love you extravagantly today in your place of need, whatever it may be.

It's true Lord that nothing is too difficult for you. Sometimes I think my ask is too big — but today you are reminding me I serve a very big God!

---

12 "Answered Prayers," *Bible Reasons*, accessed December 19, 2020, https://biblereasons.com/answered-prayers/

His Forever Love

Day Twenty-Three

"His love endures forever."

—Psalm 136:26b

Have you ever read to your children Amelia Hepworth's adorable classic children's storybook, *I Love You to the Moon and Back*? It's a delightful early childhood book depicting, through bears, the bond between a parent and child. The sun rises and a bear and her cub are beginning a day together. They do their normal, everyday activities, from splashing in the water to climbing mountains and playing with friends. They watch the colourful lights in the shimmering sky, and they share a special love language with each other—touching noses. They laugh together and hug and snuggle before bed. The story is written in very simple words that are soothing and restful.

Yesterday, as I was downsizing a bookshelf, I took the time to read the story again. A particular phrase stood out to me: "Our love is always with us, and it never, ever ends." Such a beautiful thought as the bear and cub snuggle together under the evening sky. It was a leisurely and untroubled moment—one in which I could let my imagination take me on a journey. I pictured the story rewritten with Father God and me, and I thought about my day.

Starting my day with Him, inviting Him into my every moment.

Finding the playful times—laughing with a neighbour.

Inviting His embrace during a sad moment when I was missing my kids.

Watching Him at the table during dinner, looking over my shoulder as I wondered about the $800 car repair bill.

Choosing Love

The journey was a lazy river raft ride in a summer's sun, with no one around but Him. I took time to review His whispers and let His love wash over me for those few minutes.

- *"For the Lord your God is living among you ... With his love, he will calm all your fears. He will rejoice over you with joyful songs"* (Zephaniah 3:17, NLT).
- *"... And surely I am with you always, to the very end of the age"* (Matthew 28:20b).

And then, there it was! Back from my "anointed imagining," while tucked away with Him, I knew He had just provided this encounter so that He could speak to me through that little phrase from a children's book: "Our love is always with us, and it never, ever ends." The words He highlighted at that moment were from one of my favourite passages in Romans 8:38–39:

> *... I live with the confidence that there is nothing in the universe with the power to separate us from God's love. I'm convinced that his love will triumph over death, life's troubles, fallen angels, or dark rulers in the heavens ... There is no power ... that could ever be found in the universe that can distance us from God's passionate love, which is lavished upon us through our Lord Jesus, the Anointed One!* (TPT)

Yes! You can live today knowing that your heavenly Father loves you more than you will ever understand or imagine in this lifetime. He wants to sing over you, grieve with you, laugh with you, walk with you, and nourish you with His forever love.

> *Dear Lord, I sometimes don't stop to read your love notes to me in my interactions with others, my routines, my challenges. I invite that never-ending love to nourish me today.*

The Bedrock of Love

Day Twenty-Four
Contributed by Vangie H. Price

"... choose life... make this choice by loving the Lord your God, obeying him, and committing yourself firmly to him. This is the key to your life."
—Deuteronomy 30:19–20a, NLT

Bedrock: the principles and ideas upon which something is based. Bedrock, the unshakable, immovable, unquestionable love of the Father—a depth which is unfathomable. Bedrock, the spiritual beliefs upon which my life has been stabilized.

In 1996, I collapsed into the arms of a love I'd never before experienced. In the early days of recognizing His voice, He gave me Deuteronomy 30:19–20 as a spiritual bedrock for my life. Choice is an act of selecting, or making, a decision when faced with two or more possibilities. I choose Him every day, and because I choose Him, I choose to love.

I met a girl in grade nine. A lovely friendship developed, and we wrote songs together, strumming our guitars for hours at a time. We played and sang anywhere anyone would listen, including our high school washrooms—the acoustics were amazing! JoAnne fell deeply in love with Jesus and started a Bible study in our school. She was fervent and passionate. Over the years, our lives would wind around various choices that excluded the Lover of our souls. We chose different paths, but we surfaced occasionally to speak of our latest heartbreak. We extended sympathy, bathed in alcohol, and continued on our ragged life journeys.

And then, 1996 happened. I came to the end of myself, and He was there. I chose life instead of death. I learned that amid the horrible black swirl of depression, indecision, and chaos, His clarion call lovingly pierced my heart, rubbing the sweet ointment of His peace, bringing healing to the shattered places. His love is a love that rescues. When I shared my life-changing event with JoAnne, she was silent.

I discovered that the ability to love others is completely dependent on the strength of my relationship with Him. His love for me is fierce and fiery and unrestrained. His love for me is unbounded joy. I never passed judgement, and over the next twenty-four years, I loved JoAnne consistently and authentically. I listened to her for hours, days, and years. Her life was ripped apart by broken relationships, drugs, and alcohol, but she was always open to prayer.

In October 2020, JoAnne called me from the hospital. Her neurologist had relayed bad news of a sizeable brain tumour, and she was given three to six weeks to live. When I asked her what I could do, she said, "Do what you do best, Vangie. Pray."

JoAnne requested that I act as her Power of Attorney for her health and personal care. After some thoughtful prayer, I agreed. JoAnne lived two-and-a-half hours from me, but I sensed God's voice speaking and pressing me forward. His deep love that I had experienced for so long in my own journey was available and ready for pouring out. When she was moved to a hospice setting, I didn't leave her side. Two days before she was carried away on angel wings, she sat up in bed and asked, "Am I dying?" I held her ever so tightly and said, "Yes, JoAnne. We all have to go on this journey—but you are not alone." I was absolutely assured by the presence of His peace and hers that she had made her choice to live eternally with her Saviour and the Lover of her soul, to whom she had returned.

Holy Spirit, thank you for the moments in our lives, though difficult, when we can observe your love bringing forgiveness and healing to the ready heart. What joy to know your love, which will chase a wandering one down to the end of their days. Set me on the bedrock of your truth and love.

You've Always Loved

Day Twenty-Five
Contributed by Jacqueline Angi-Dobos

"Your unfailing love, O Lord, is as vast as the heavens; your faithfulness reaches beyond the clouds."

—Psalm 36:5, NLT

The song "You've Always Loved," written by Abby Clattenberg, resonates through me when I think of how much God protected me on October 31, 2020. "Oh Father, you've always been there, and you've always loved" plays over and over in my mind when I share my story with others. "I will praise you all my days."[13]

That Saturday began with a relaxing brunch with friends. Then I turned my focus to a task awaiting me in my back yard—a massive tree limb needed to be removed. The last strong windstorm had convinced me that it couldn't wait.

After a trip to the hardware store, I headed back home with everything I would need. The knowledgeable young man who served me in the rental department directed me to a small electric chainsaw rather than the huge gas run one I was considering. As I look back, I see that even in gathering the equipment, the Lord's love was in full operation. I was fully prepared with safety equipment, and the ladder I was using firmly fastened to the tree. Yes, I felt a bit uneasy as I climbed fifteen feet up to begin the task. In the back of my mind, I thought that I should actually leave the job until I could rent a safety harness, but I pushed that thought away, as I wanted to get the job done and move on to other things.

---

13 Abby Clattenberg, "You've Always Loved," 2016, Lakemount Worship Centre. Used with permission.

Unknown to me, God had set other things in place. My daughter, inside working on her university course, left her online class and came outside to watch. Paramedics were nearby. The ladder was new and strong, but stronger still was the Lord's unfailing and vigilant watch of love over me.

The saw was purring, and it seemed that success was in sight. Suddenly, I stopped cutting as dread filled me—I realized I had forgotten to make an undercut. Time stood still as the massive limb began it's near lethal swing, smashing into my foot and knocking me off the ladder. I crashed to the ground, flat on my back.

The next few minutes were a blur as my daughter rushed to my side and summoned the nearby paramedics. They stabilized me with a neck brace and a backboard—all the while watching the massive limb wedged in the firmly fastened ladder suspended directly above us!

Did that promised, unfailing love prevent the accident entirely? No! Yet I praise Him that I was spared so much of what "could have happened." My foot wasn't broken, nor was my neck or my back! I'm amazed that even though the weeks ahead in my healing journey included dealing with three broken ribs and a broken sternum, I'm alive and more than ready to glorify God for His divine intervention.

Blessings awaited me through the support of family, friends, and colleagues. Their multiplied kindnesses were expressions of the Lord's unfailing love. We are assured of God's presence even in times of pain and difficulties. It's true: His faithfulness reaches us with preserving power. "You've Always Loved" is more than a song; it's who He is.

Oh Father, you've always been there, and You've always loved. Jesus, each day with you is an adventure. Sometimes, I admit, I don't get things perfectly aligned with your "best" plans for me. But I'm so thankful that you are my protector, my source of healing and strength, and the one who holds my future in your hands.

A Father's Love

Day Twenty-Six

"From a long distance away, his father saw him coming, dressed as a beggar, and great compassion swelled up in his heart for his son who was returning home. So the father raced out to meet him. He swept him up in his arms, hugged him dearly, and kissed him over and over with tender love."

—Luke 15:20, TPT

From the day they knew he was to be born, they had awaited his birth with expectation and pride. A son—and a new brother. The depth of love only grew in the father's heart as he watched him grow and learn the family business. But now his heart was breaking as he observed the growing turbulence in this younger son's soul. There had been signs of restlessness, rebellion, and disrespect. The need for independence and immediate gratification had been persistent. He could not bring harmony between the two boys, and the outflowing of love and wisdom was met by the younger son with disdain and threats.

Now he was asking for his inheritance. To request an early inheritance was as good as wishing one's father dead. The arrow of rejection hit hard. It seemed irrational and arrogant, especially when the farm was thriving and he lacked nothing—but the father saw no reason to withhold the inheritance from him.

Once the inheritance had been acquired, this wild and demanding son gathered up his belongings and took off to "enjoy life," leaving his big brother behind to run the family business with his father. There were obvious clues to indicate that this departure wasn't reason for rejoicing. The father didn't know where his son was going. The son hadn't been schooled in managing "the streets." His impetuous nature, his lack of loyalty, and his unteachable character made it clear that he didn't have a plan and he didn't seem to care. This wasn't what the father had planned for this son he loved. He had dreams for him that were grand and glorious.

The throbbing pain in his heart was undeniable, and day after day the father felt that wound of rejection from the son—the choice he had made for something other than his father's unfailing love. Underneath, he knew there was nothing his son could ever do, or fail to do, that would keep him from his father's love. He was his son. He would wait with patience, investing faith, hope, and expectation for that day of his prodigal's return.

Many days of riotous living passed before the son came to his senses. With a repentant heart, he made his way home. When the son was still a long way down the road, his grace-filled father ran to meet him. There was no question of his love and forgiveness—it was conspicuous and extravagant. Even the complaints and jealousy of the older brother wouldn't mar this homecoming reunion.

There are many lessons to be gleaned from this parable of the prodigal son in Luke 15. In an entire lifetime, we're not likely to fully understand just how much God loves and treasures us as His sons and daughters. We can't even faintly fathom the extent of the grace, patience, and love that He extends to us. When we choose to take detours of disobedience, complacency, doubt, or independence on our personal journeys, He waits for us with love. He never throws away the great plans and purposes He has for us, but He guards them, awaiting our return.

As we consider the father's welcome back of the prodigal, let's consider the blessing and joy that are ours as part of God's family. Let's appreciate His consistent loving response to our repentance. Let's stay close, serve Him well, return our love to Him, and be renewed in His presence. There's nothing better than to be at home in the Father's embrace.

Father God, you have called me yours, and I sense again the depth of your love. Forgive me for the times when I've distanced myself from you through foolish choices. Hold me tight. I receive your forgiveness and your eternal love.

Dr. Luke's Lesson on Love (with a Twist)

Day Twenty-Seven

Contributed by Doris Rome

"'So which of these ... do you think was neighbor....?'And he said, 'He who showed mercy on him.' Then Jesus said to him, 'Go and do likewise.'"
—Luke 10:36–37, NKJV

How well I remember standing at the front door waving and crying as my husband, Ken, and two children, Paul and Ruth, left for church that morning. I hadn't felt well for four months, but today was the worst. My strength was beyond depleted. By Monday morning, I was dealing with a knee that was swollen to double its size, and movement was difficult. I called my doctor again, this time for a referral to a specialist. He agreed to consider it but wanted to re-examine first.

Responding in a much more decisive manner at this point, he arranged for me to be hospitalized immediately, citing either rheumatic fever or rheumatoid arthritis as the likely culprit. Ken was out of town with his work, and the children were at school. Getting to the hospital would require some help. Without hesitation, my sister-in-law, Audrey, in Woodstock came to transport me. She would then wait at the apartment for the children until Ken got home. What a blessing of love and kindness she was!

At the same time as I was met with these health challenges, I was enrolled in a course at church entitled, "How to Love Your Neighbour!" I was so excited to put learning into practice... but now this. My ability to participate had just been abruptly halted! And then it all began to unfold before me, scene after scene.

- My pastor visited, and the prayer line family at our church offered to pray ... and pray they did!
- My neighbours and family helped to care for my children.
- My "secret sister" dropped off numerous "cheer up surprises."
- Ken came home often to a lovingly prepared hot meal delivered to the door, and friends invited the family for special Easter meals.
- Beautiful cards and notes arrived each day from my church family, neighbours, and friends. They meant so much!
- Visitors came—over one hundred in eighteen days!

Somewhere along the line, I got it! It was a "Love Your Neighbour" course unfolding in real life, and I was the recipient, the audience watching the production of Heaven's beautiful sacrificial, humble, compassionate love delivered by God's servants!

While I was recovering, He gave me some simple "practice" opportunities to reach out that would work from my place of confinement. I was invited at various times to read my Bible aloud for another patient. My daily devotions and prayer times were welcomed by my roommate, whose only son seldom visited—so I shared my pastor with her. The prayers and praise that she heard from my bedside were used by God to bring her truth and hope. Only five days later, she left that bed for eternity. Yes, there were little acts of love I could distribute as I healed.

After eighteen days, I left that hospital room well trained by these abundant blessings of heartfelt love showered on me, and I was determined to put into practice the instruction to "Go and do likewise!"

Jesus, you do surprise us many times with your outpoured love. Keep teaching me to be a good "receiver" of the acts of love that others bring to my life. Make me an instrument of your love to those I meet in my journey. I want to love them in the same caring and attentive manner in which you have loved me. Amen.

Love Sees More

Day Twenty-Eight

"... that old way of life has to go ... take on an entirely new way of life—a God-fashioned life ... as God accurately reproduces his character in you."
—Ephesians 4:23–24 MSG

I have always loved the New Testament parables. I love that Jesus used everyday events, nature, and relationships to teach such valuable lessons. They have been described as metaphors or similes that arrest the hearer by their vividness or strangeness. There's the new wine in old wineskins, the wise and foolish builders, the sower and the seeds, the lost coin, the mustard seed, the lost sheep, the grey blanket, and more. If you see one there that doesn't sound familiar, stay tuned.

Revelation 21:5 says, *"I am making everything new!"* New has many meanings, including something never before seen, or something discovered or seen for the first time. It can mean something freshly attempted or something replacing the former, such as a new teacher. It can also mean something introduced, such as a new vaccine or a new Xbox game. For the most part, "new" excites me—a new book, a new class, a new project, a new vacation destination. Isn't it amazing that our God, who is the same yesterday, today, and tomorrow, is at the same time making all things new!

Newness takes me back to the kitchen table in my childhood home. Our home was mother's workshop of love. Many transformations took place on the kitchen table. Old match boxes were glued together to fashion tiny storage drawers a step ahead of Rubbermaid. Cards were made for missionaries, buttons were sorted for future use and then carded by colour, and the list goes on.

Mom was always busy sewing. Material was expensive, but Mom found a variety of ways around it. On every bed there were two or three heavy quilted grey blankets, which, as they wore down, became the material for new creations. At the kitchen table, she would lay out the most holey and worn of the blankets, and wiggle some patterns around on them to salvage the best parts. Before you knew it, new coats and hats for the four of us would emerge.

I have always thought of the story of the grey blankets as a present-day parable right up there next to the "real" ones. You see, just like Jesus was hiding a deeper lesson in His parables, there was one here. When Jesus chose disciples, He chose people who could be changed by His love, people would be willing to be set out on His kitchen table, reshaped, trimmed here and there, and made into something wonderful. Then He sent them out to communicate that His acceptance was available to anyone—even to those whose lives were marked by wear and tear, over-use, and failure.

We may wonder what Jesus sees in us when He calls us to be His disciples. But we must believe that He loves us and accepts us, and He still has a new and wonderful plan for us that we may not have yet realized. His twelve disciples were all in the midst of regular routine—fishermen, political activists, tax collectors, uncommon leaders, rich and poor, educated and uneducated. God uses ordinary people just like you and me to do His extraordinary work and share His love and truth.

His invitation to us is adventurous and grace-filled. But it is a choice. Are we willing to offer ourselves to his reshaping and trimming and the discovery of something new? *His love sees more*, and it's His offer to you. If you're willing, climb up on His table and prepare for transformation.

Father, it feels a little unsettling to imagine something so different that you may want to do with me. But my heart fills with anticipation that you see something amazing that I haven't yet imagined. I'm willing, with your help and your grace. Let's get started! Amen.

Held by Love

Day Twenty-Nine
Contributed by Rachelle Mainse

"Love never stops loving."

—1 Corinthians 13:8a, TPT

I always get a look of surprise when someone asks me where I was born and I tell them Australia. I wasn't supposed to be born in Brisbane; my parents certainly weren't expecting me when they travelled from Canada to minister at Expo '88. But three-and-a-half months early, I arrived with the doctors saying I only had a 15 per cent chance of living. What was supposed to be a two-week trip turned into four long, terrifying months for my parents.

Most babies experience the kisses, cuddles, and warmth of their parents' arms when they're born. I experienced trauma and the warmth of an incubator. My parents weren't allowed to touch me for a long time. Plastic walls separated us. As they looked through them daily, they heard my cries and saw the pain on my face as I got pricked with needles. They saw my struggle, discomfort, and pain as the feeding tube tape got ripped from my skin and a new tube pushed through my nasal passage into my stomach once again. As much as I hurt, I know my parents hurt even more seeing their baby go through so much suffering. From dawn to dusk, they would stay at the hospital—until literally the staff would make them leave. They prayed, they cried, they waited, they watched … and most of all, they loved.

Thirty-two years later, it's clear to me that more than the kisses, cuddles, and hugs that I later experienced, this extremely dark and painful time in my life most demonstrated to me my parents' love for me.

I believe love is shown infinitely more in the hard times than in the good. I may have not been held by physical arms, as most children are at the start of their life, but oh, I was held. I was held by love every step of the way.

In some of the most challenging times of my life, God has reminded me of the story of my birth and my parents' love as an illustration of His love and care for me. How amazing to think that as great as my parents' example is, it doesn't even come close to God.

Maybe you feel you're in the "fight of your life." Maybe you feel all alone. Maybe you daily feel pricked with pain or the tearing of your heart. Maybe you're wondering, "Where is God?" I want to encourage you that, although you may not feel Him, see Him, or understand what's going on or why, God's right there. Perhaps you'll find yourself one day saying that the most painful time has become the most evident reminder of God's love demonstrated for you.

Be encouraged. He's watching over you 24/7. He's with you through every bump of the ride. No "hospital staff" can kick Him out. He says, "I'm rooting for you. I've got you. I'm not letting go." The Bible says His love never fails (I Corinthians 13:8). That word "fails" in the Greek means to "fall." His love is never going to falter … come undone … change. He's with you through it all—regardless! This includes the messes of our own making!

No one may know how dark the night is, and there might not be physical arms to hold you, but know this—you are being held. He's never left your side, and He's fighting for you in ways you can't see or understand right now. And although it might look dark, His love has never dimmed: "Love never stops loving" (I Corinthians 13:8, TPT).

Jesus, your love never stops. I'm so thankful that you are rooting for me. Your love is so much greater than even the best that I have known, and when life is painful and fragile, you remain my safety and my strength. I'm choosing your life-giving, restorative, and unrestricted love today.

The Father Stepped In

Day Thirty
Contributed by Peggy Kennedy

"See what great love the Father has lavished on us, that we should be called children of God!"

—I John 3:1

The Father stepped in! And with that action, the future of the newborn son was redirected. What a traumatic day it was for Jacob and his family. We read of this day in Genesis 35:13–18. They had just had a divine encounter at Bethel, where the Lord had spoken with Jacob. The familiar anticipation of childbirth permeated the atmosphere. It would be Rachel's second child, and delivery day had arrived. As they paused on their journey from Bethel to Ephrath, they soon realized all was not well. It wasn't just a "difficult childbirth," but it was the day Rachel would breathe her last breath. The attending midwives attempted to bring her joy by declaring that she had given birth to a son; however, in her dying breath, filled with pain and grief, she released the words that named her son. She named him "Ben Oni," the "son of my sorrow," imposing on her newborn a negative identity. To all who knew the meaning, they would know that the future of the child would be shaped by that name: "son of my sorrow." But everything changed in that dismal hour when Jacob *stepped in* and assigned a new name and a new future: *Benjamin*, which means "son of my right hand."

We know from the record of scripture that this name spoke of a position of preference, strength, honour, and power. It spoke of being valued and treasured, and even of authority. What a glorious contrast!

Many generations later when Benjamin's descendants were about to enter the promised land, Moses prophesied over these offspring who would now gain their inheritance: *"About Benjamin he said: 'Let the beloved of the Lord rest secure in him, for he shields him all day long, and the one the Lord loves rests between his shoulders"* (Deuteronomy 33:12). What a picture of protective love that even warriors need!

As we come to the end of our study, do you see how those words *"the father stepped in"* reveal to us a picture of the love of the heavenly Father for each of us? The story of the Bible from Genesis onward tells us that, through disobedience, sin entered the entire human race. We were born into what is even worse than "sorrow." We were born in sin and had no way to save ourselves. Yet the same story from cover-to-cover reveals that the Father *stepped in* and so loved the world—so loved us—that He sent His Son. Oh, what a lavish love. He gave His *one* Son that we could become the privileged sons and daughters with a future that extends all the way into eternal life.

The cross is the ultimate picture of the lavish love of the heavenly Father. I required that love for both my salvation and my destiny. I needed the Father to step into my story—each of us does! Strength, value, and a preferred position are made possible for each of us as His beloved sons and daughters. He stepped in for you. Now you can step into what His lavish love holds in store for you as you continue your journey.

> *Father, you have, with your love, stepped into my life! May I be ever mindful of the cross and the radically victorious new life and destiny you have provided. May the outflowing of your love in me be expressed to others in selflessness, servanthood, humility, compassion, patience, and sacrifice. In Jesus' name, Amen.*

Small Group Helps

This devotional journey welcomes the participation of others in a small group setting, either in person or online. A four-week group session, meeting once weekly, is recommended. Each participant will need their own copy of the book and can journal any take-aways or questions from their daily readings. In a small group setting, all participants should be reading the devotional entries at the same time so that discussions centre around the same readings on any given week. Discussing your insights will reveal some impacting and exciting truths.

The group leader may select two to five questions from the following list for the weekly group meeting, which should run between sixty and seventy-five minutes. Vary your selection of questions from the list, adapting them to your group's focus. Be sure to allow time for personal thoughts, testimonies of growth, and any questions. Keep a scriptural view as foundational and expect God to meet with you as you gather. The preferred leadership style for this topic is facilitation, where the leader encourages both participation and time boundaries during sharing. The facilitator should be familiar with the material and keep the discussion moving.

Discussion Questions (Choose Your Own Adventure!)

1. Which biblical character or event was most impactful to your growth this week?
2. What life lesson did you learn from that character or event?

3. Which testimony stood out for you this week? Share what you gained from it.
4. Share one truth or lesson that might be relevant to pass along to a specific friend in the near future.
5. Choose a scripture verse from this week's devotionals and unpack what it means in your life right now.
6. Talk about the most difficult time you needed to show love. Allow the group to pray for you. (One or two each week could do this.)
7. Which relational struggle (i.e. unforgiveness, jealousy, resentment, injustice, unfairness, negativity, gossip, belittlement, rejection, control, ingratitude, etc.) prevents you from loving and why?
8. Jesus is always ready to help us, but we must be willing to ask. What is your most difficult ask when it comes to love and why?
9. Comment on this statement: "If I could really believe He loved me as much as the Bible says, I think I would be less insecure."
10. How do you "refill"?
11. Is forgiveness a key to loving that you haven't utilized well? Who do you need to forgive?
12. God wants us to love selflessly. To what degree are we hoping for reciprocal love?
13. If God spoke to you today about freedom from your fears and limitations about showing love, what would He be saying to you? What would the new you look like?
14. In what area of your life do you need more love?
15. How are you making room for His presence like the Shunamite woman did?
16. What are some of the negative thought patterns or judgements that need to change in your life? Listen to the Holy Spirit and suggest some new truths and declarations that He is directing you to make.
17. Keep a list of wins this week in the area of love and be ready to share some of those wins next week.

18. Where has God used you in the past few weeks to impart love into a situation?
19. Come next week with a scripture that expresses God's love for you and tell what it means to you.
20. What are some key rewards for loving from the heart?
21. Have you ever loved and lost? How is that still affecting your decisions?
22. What would it mean for you to get up on God's "kitchen table" and let Him remake you?
23. Have you ever received an outpouring of love financially, like Sulojana, and what did that mean to you?
24. Have you ever had to do some heavy lifting to show love for a friend? Share with the group.
25. Share with the group what your alabaster time looks like. What have you found helpful in pouring out your love?
26. How does the concept of letting go apply to your intimacy with Jesus?
27. Share a testimony of how "the Father stepped in" for you.
28. Have you had the privilege of being the recipient of affirming love, like Sandra? Share with the group.
29. What does Wendy's story say to you personally about obedience and love?

If the group would like to add a summary week (a fifth week), we suggest each participant come with a brief testimony related to their growth and revelation in this journey toward abundant love and that the group give time to celebration and prayer for one another. Be sure to invite all group members to experience personal salvation and have a time of prayer for those they love.

Note: As a bonus, for the first eighteen months after release, contact the author at ruth.teakle@gmail.com to have one of the contributors as a guest (online only) at one of your group sessions. Details upon request.

Choosing Love: My Notes

Choosing Love: My Notes

Contributors

Jacqueline Angi-Dobos (nee Rawlinson) has been serving the Lord since her salvation encounter with Him in 1985 while in her third year of university. Her journey has included some exciting and fulfilling time as a missionary in Spain and in Hungary. Jacqueline has worked at Niagara Christian Collegiate in Fort Erie, Ontario as the Director of International Education since 2010. She, her husband, and daughter reside in St. Catharines, Ontario, and she serves her home church in the area of missions and prayer.

Crystal Barley is the proud momma of Judah, Isaac, and Ezra. She's one of the associate pastors at Coastal Church in Daphne, Alabama and has been involved in church ministry for fourteen years. God has used her testimony of healing, forgiveness, and Christ-centred identity as a platform to preach His gospel across nations. She has a passion to see this generation fully receive Christ, find their voice, and, like John the Baptist, prepare the way of the Lord's coming!

Heather Bennett-Chamberlain is a mom to three amazing kids: Sadie, Lucy, and Garrison. She's been married for almost twenty years to her wonderful husband, Jesse. She has lived in Grimsby most of her life and currently resides in historic Grimsby Beach. Heather serves on staff at Lakemount Worship Centre, assisting the Connections Pastor. In her spare time, Heather loves to get lost in history and fabric.

Shelly Calcagno is a freelance writer and producer from the Niagara Region. She studied English Literature at Brock University and Religious Education at Master's College and Seminary. She followed that with twenty years of pastoral church ministry to children and families. Shelly loves to write, speak, and blog, and she has self-published a children's book, *Tini's Tangles*. In 2020, she started a pandemic-launched podcast called *A Space for Grace*. Shelly loves DIY projects, working the garden, and drinking coffee! She is passionate about legacy and bringing ideas to life. Shelly is married and has two awesome young adult children.

"Sandy" Courtney grew up in Caledon East, Ontario. When she married, she moved to Orangeville, Ontario, where she and her husband, Joe, raised their two children, Jennifer and Joey, who have given them four grandchildren. Sandra loves the outdoors and could challenge the best in a good day of fishing. She now resides in Listowel, Ontario, where she assists Joe with their business, Courtney Auctions. Sandra and Joe serve together in prayer ministry at Crossroads Life Church in Harriston, Ontario.

Laurie Florek was employed by Westinghouse, Hamilton until she got married in 1959. She boasts three beautiful children from that union and two who were blended in from a second marriage in 1985. Laurie's career was in Human Resources, and her hobbies have included reading and knitting. She has served in an outstanding manner for many years in weekly prison ministry through her home church.

Contributors

Wendy Hagar, Founder and Executive Director of Sew on Fire Ministries, has given this ministry leadership for over twenty years. It's her joy to direct this 100 per cent volunteer international humanitarian organization, sending aid to over one hundred countries. In 2011, Wendy was the recipient of Burlington's Citizen of the Year, and in 2012, the Queen Elizabeth II Diamond Jubilee Medal. She has also been honoured with the Paul Harris Community Award by Rotary groups in Waterdown and Burlington. Wendy and her husband, Jeff, reside in Ontario. Their two children, Matt and Sarah, have given them six adorable GrandJoys. Wendy loves spending time with her family, camping, swimming, baking, and doing crafts with her grandchildren.

www.sewonfire.com

Jenna Harmon lives in the Niagara region of Ontario where she is a pastor's wife and stay-at-home mother of two beautiful boys, Moses and Shepard. She enjoys spending her time working with special needs children, cleaning, organizing her house, and shopping online. Jenna is passionate about raising men of character and ministering alongside her husband at their local church.

Rev. Peggy Kennedy together with her husband, Jack, form the Two Silver Trumpets Ministries. As their name from Numbers 10 indicates, they minister to leaders and across the body of Christ in Canada and internationally. In addition to active pulpit ministry, Peggy is the author of three books: *A Is for Apple*, *Hear the Sound*, and *Chosen—Conversations of God with His Mighty Warrior*, as well as numerous teaching manuals. When Peggy isn't on the road, she serves her home church with excellence in ministry eldership, prayer, and prophetic encouragement.

www.TwoSilverTrumpets.ca

Rachelle Mainse is an entrepreneur, writer, and speaker who resides in Texas. Her friendship with God and her heart for preteen girls led her to develop an exceptional mentorship curriculum, Princess911, specifically for that age group. Her priority interests include family, travel, the dog she doesn't yet own, and inspiring others through her writing and speaking.

@RachelleMainse | www.Princess911.com

Vangie Price was born into a busy ministry household in Belleville, Ontario, to parents who were lovers of Jesus, pioneers, and builders. After attending Bible college in her late teens, she married and gave birth to a beautiful son, an amazing daughter, and another baby whom she will meet in heaven. Following a painful divorce, her life spiraled downwards, and addiction became part of her story. Seventeen years later, she was captivated by Jesus and has never looked back. Although she wears professional Addiction and Mental Health hats, Vangie oozes with passion in serving the Lord. She enjoys rich friendships, and her children and grandchildren bring her delight.

Doris Rome has always had two loves: the Lord and her family. She has served the Lord with gladness in whatever capacity became open to her, including Sunday school teacher and superintendent, seniors and shut-ins visitation, and hospitality. Doris is best known across Canada as a valued speaker at women's conventions and conferences, and as a faithful leader in PAOC women's ministry. She was pianist and band member for thirty years and continues to play at her seniors' home. Doris was married to her late husband, Ken, for fifty-eight years and has two children, five grandchildren, and seven great grandchildren, who are the joy of her life.

Sulojana Sam lives in St. Catharines, Ontario, where she works full-time for the Government of Canada. She and her husband, Jeeva, a retired pastor, have founded a ministry to mentor married couples from the brink of breakdown to breakthrough in as little as ten weeks (www.thesams.ca). Sulojana expresses her passion for helping the less fortunate and evangelism by volunteering at the Niagara Dream Centre. She also started and co-leads a prayer/Bible study group at her workplace. Jeeva and Sulojana are parents of three grown children: Priya, Sathiya, and Jaya. Sathiya is married to Shaloma, and the other two are engaged.

About the Author

Ruth Teakle lives with her husband, Carl, in Beamsville, Ontario. She loves to spend time with her three children and their spouses and her eleven grandchildren. Although retired, Ruth serves as a support staff member at Lakemount Worship Centre in Grimsby, Ontario, where she previously served on full-time and part-time staff for eighteen years. Her roles varied from overseeing small groups and missions to prayer and pastoral care. As well, she has led and assisted with numerous short-term missions to the Caribbean, Eastern Europe, Ukraine, South America, northern Ontario, and Quebec.

On the home front, Ruth and Carl have fostered over 130 children during a twenty-five-year period. Ruth has worked within the Correctional Services of Canada, led numerous summer camp programs through both Girls Guides of Canada and the Salvation Army, directed an annual city-wide Christmas toy program, and filmed a national training course for telephone prayer partners.

Ruth's academic pursuits have included studies at Lakeshore Teachers' College, Brock University (Bachelor of Arts), and Wagner University (Master of Practical Ministries). She has completed ESL studies and is a Certified Anger Management Specialist. Prior to taking additional Religious Studies courses with Global University in preparation for ordained ministry, Ruth enjoyed a successful thirty-two-year career as an elementary school teacher.

Ruth's heart is to see people become passionate followers of Christ. She has a strong sense of mission to help people build healthy connections with God and others and walk in the fullness of their destiny. Her challenging but victorious personal journey makes her well qualified to share on the joy of living in His agape love in this fourth devotional, *Choosing Love*.

Additional Note: Ruth's first devotional, *Changing Seasons*, is a pocket/purse sized devotional full of encouragement from God's Word written especially for seniors, and it's one of the GODQUEST SERIES available only through The Bible League, Canada. bibleleague.ca/resources/godquest/

Pursuing Patience, Pursuing Peace, and *Choosing Love* are available through Word Alive Press and numerous national and international outlets.

Ruth has also authored a delightfully illustrated children's book for children ages four to nine, *Joshua Wonders: What Does the Tooth Fairy Do with My Teeth?* available through numerous national and international outlets.